Swing Trading

the Beginner's Guide on How to Trade for Profits with the Best Strategies and Technical Analysis. You will Find Inside the A-Z Glossary to All Technical Terms Used

I0499892

Written By

Nathan Real

© Copyright 2019 - All rights reserved.

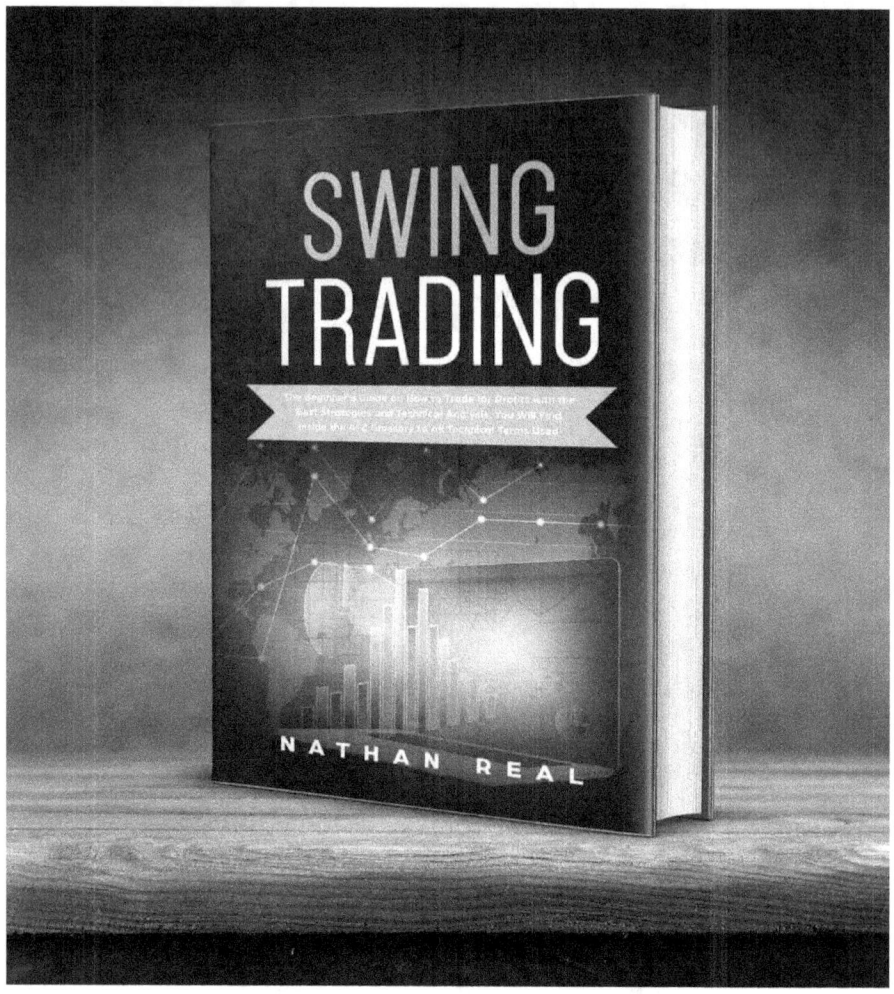

The content contained within this book may not be reproduced, duplicated or transmitted without direct written permission from the author or the publisher.

Under no circumstances will any blame or legal responsibility be held against the publisher, or author, for any damages, reparation, or monetary loss due to the information contained within this book. Either directly or indirectly.

Legal Notice:

This book is copyright protected. This book is only for personal use. You cannot amend, distribute, sell, use, quote or paraphrase any part, or the content within this book, without the consent of the author or publisher.

Disclaimer Notice:

Please note the information contained within this document is for educational and entertainment purposes only. All effort has been executed to present accurate, up to date, and reliable, complete information. No warranties of any kind are declared or implied. Readers acknowledge that the author is not engaging in the rendering of legal, financial, medical or professional advice. The content within this book has been derived from various sources. Please consult a licensed professional before attempting any techniques outlined in this book.

By reading this document, the reader agrees that under no circumstances is the author responsible for any losses, direct or indirect, which are incurred as a result of the use of information contained within this document, including, but not limited to, — errors, omissions, or inaccuracies.

Table of Contents

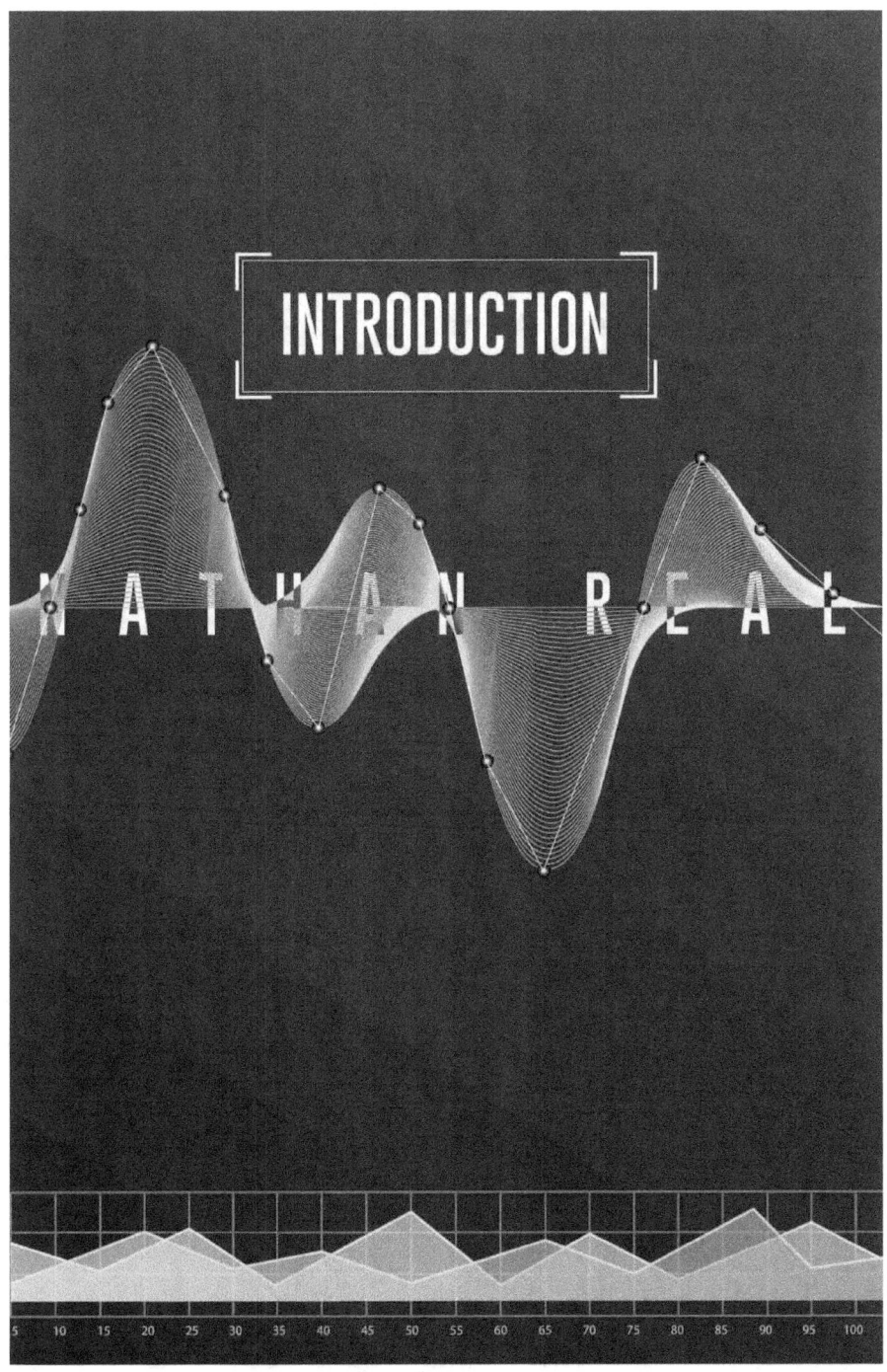

INTRODUCTION

NATHAN REAL

Introduction

These days, the only thing you need to become a trader is a computer and good internet access. As a result, the number of people trading in the stock market has grown significantly in the past few years. The average Joe can take advantage of the opportunities available on the stock market to make a profit from the movement in stock prices.

There is also a much wider array of resources available to the prospective stock trader. Within a matter of minutes, I could access several websites and videos offering me stock strategies from experienced traders. It has never been easier to educate yourself and enter the market as a trader. I can keep informed in real-time about the stock market from the grocery store or the beach using only my cell phone. As a trader its important to have information readily available so that you can respond to changes in the market and make a profit.

But what is trading? We often hear about people trading on the stock market, but what does this mean? How do people make a profit simply by buying and selling shares and stocks, and what are their strategies? How do they know which stocks to choose and which trends to watch? A trader makes money by taking advantage of the upward and downward movements of stock prices. The simplest breakdown of trading is 'buy low and sell high'. This is how traders make a profit in the stock market. But you will learn that there is much more to it than that. There are other tools and methods that traders use. Understanding these tools requires an understanding of different types of markets.

Usually, when we refer to the market in this book, we are talking about the stock market. If you aren't very experienced in trading, then this is probably the market you are most familiar with. There are many other kinds of markets where traders buy and sell to make a profit. When we refer to the stock market, we are talking about the market where shares in companies are sold. These are often referred to as securities. When you buy a stock, you are buying a certain percentage of ownership of that company. When the value of the company increases; the value of your share of ownership will increase. If the value of the company decreases, then your percentage of ownership will hold less value.

The value of the company is mainly determined by the company's success and profitability. But there are other factors which affect the value of a company's stock. The overall performance of the economy can affect the performance of an individual company. A company might be extremely profitable, but suddenly they are involved in a scandal or a major lawsuit which causes the price of shares to go down. A good trader will keep track of these factors in order to monitor the health of their stocks.

As a trader, you should think of owning a share as if you are the owner of a business. Famed investor and hedge fund manager have said that when you are considering purchasing a stock, you should treat it as if you are considering purchasing the entire business. If you were going to buy a business, think about what types of questions you would ask beforehand. What would you want to know about the person managing the business? Do they have the experience and skills necessary, and would you trust them with your hard-earned capital? What kind of product or service does the company provide? Think about the long-term prospects of that company and whether the company is doing a good job of staying relevant in the ever-changing world. Of course, you also want to know if the company is making a profit. When you buy a business, after all, you buy it with the expectation that it will make you a profit. You should buy shares of a company with the same mindset.

In addition to trading shares in companies, people can also trade raw materials. The materials we use to build houses or consumer products also have a value that is determined by a market and influencing economic factors. Raw material like steel doesn't always trade for the same price. A shortage of machinery or a rise in the cost of steel production will affect the price of steel. Companies who produce consumer goods are constantly dealing with the rise and fall of the cost of raw materials and these changes will affect how much they are able to produce at a given time. If the price of steel goes up, then construction costs will also increase. Traders can make money by anticipating these changes in the price of raw materials. This is known as the commodities market. Traders on the commodities market buy some amount of raw materials, usually on paper through a brokerage firm, anticipating that at some point that raw material will be valued higher and they can capitalize on the price discrepancy. A brief glimpse at a chart of the price of steel over the last year won't look much different from a chart showing the price of a stock or a security index; it will be made up of peaks and values where the price of that raw material has risen and fallen over time depending on external factors.

While the technical aspects of commodities trading are similar, a trader in commodities must pay attention to different indicators than someone who trades in stocks and securities. Where a stock trader might watch for news about a certain company and the development of their products, a commodities trader might keep a close eye on steel manufacturing firms and their levels of production, or how import and export taxes are affecting oil companies in the Persian Gulf.

When we buy stocks in a company then we are also buying the risks associated with owning that business. I could open a business today, and five years from now the business could be worth significantly more money. The business could also go bankrupt after six months, which means I would lose all the capital I invested in the business. Traders should never forget this when they are considering buying a share in a company. Remember to treat it like you are buying the whole business. The business could be profitable, but it could also lose money which means that you will lose money.

Most traders will mitigate the risk by not pouring all their capital in one stock. By investing all your money in one company then theoretically you would make more money if that stock did very well. But, if you put all your money in one company and the company goes bankrupt, then you'll lose the entirety of your investment. Instead, traders diversify. If I had $1000 dollars to invest, rather than taking $1000 dollars and placing my faith in one company I would be better off breaking that $1000 dollar up, putting $100 into ten different stocks.

Companies sell stocks as a method of generating capital for growing their business. Businesses need liquid cash to operate, meaning they need the money that isn't tied up or committed to other expenses. A company that wants to expand will issue stocks in the hopes that people will buy them, resulting in cash flow that the company can reinvest into developing new products.

People choose to invest in the stock market as an alternative to saving money in the bank. By putting your money in the stock market and leaving it long term, you are letting your money 'work' over time so that you make more money. Banks try to encourage saving by paying members interest rates. A bank makes a profit by lending money from the pool of its member's money. In return for putting your money in the bank and allowing it to do lend your money to other people, they pay you an interest rate. Interest rates used to be a good incentive for people to save their money in banks. If they put money in the bank, then the value of their money would grow over time with interest rates. Nowadays, interest rates that banks provide are typically too low to even beat the inflation rate which means that if you're keeping your money in the bank long term then your money is losing a small amount of value.

To understand this, you must understand how inflation works. Over time the price of products and services slowly increases. People's wages ideally increase to keep up with the rate of inflation, so that they can still afford a consistent level of goods and services. The downside of keeping your money in a bank account long-term is that the interest rate you receive from the bank won't keep up with the inflation rate. If the price of goods and services rises on average by 2% over the next year, but the bank only pays you .25% interest, then the actual value of your money has gone down. This means that you'll be able to buy fewer goods and services with the same amount of money in the future.

The advantage of investing is that even if you are a long-term, low-risk investor, your money will grow at a rate that keeps up with the rate of inflation. If the inflation rate over the next ten years averages at 2%, and you have a well-diversified portfolio of stocks that returns about 8% per year, then you're beating the inflation rate and making profit. You're not only increasing the dollar amount of your money; the actual value of your money is increasing.

Diversifying your portfolio profit can play a huge role in reducing your risk, especially if you are a long-term investor. While the stock market may have periods of time where it drops in value, the historical trend for the entire stock market is a gradual increase year after year. If you diversify your investments, you might have one or two investments that don't do as well or even perform poorly. However, you can expect the cumulative trend of your stocks to be an increase if you've diversified properly and chosen stocks in reliable companies.

While many people have a perception of the stock market as a place where you can get rich overnight, this requires a mindset that is somewhat akin to gambling. To be a successful investor or trader, you must put in a good amount of work evaluating companies and choosing the right time to buy a stock or enter a market. The one thing this book will not do is teach you how to get rich quick, or how to make money quickly. This book will, however, give you tools to begin trading with well thought out strategies. You will also learn how to minimize risk so that you can profit from your good trades while minimizing losses when you make a bad trade.

This book will cover one of the specific trading mindsets among a wide variety of approaches. This type of trading is known as swing trading. It's a trading that is differentiated by the time frame and the strategies used when a trader is approaching the market. There are three main categories that traders and investors typically fall in to; there is the day trader, the swing trader, and the long-term position trader. While each of these different types of traders will compete in the same markets, the strategies and approaches that they use will differ. They might buy and sell the same securities and commodities even; but the indicators that they will watch for will be different, the signs for when to 'buy' and when to 'sell' will vary.

An average Joe like you and I would be called a retail trader. When we trade on the stock market, we aren't doing it for a firm or a financial agency. Our investing efforts aren't part of a corporate finance plan and we don't run a hedge fund. These people would be referred to as institutional traders. Warren Buffet would be considered an institutional trader because private investors entrust him with their money, and he invests it for them. In order to be an institutional trader, you must meet certain criteria and have the right qualifications. Most of the stock market is comprised of the institutional traders who manage hedge funds and mutual funds. Compared to institutional traders, you or I would be considered small fish. Our volumes are considerably lower. We own less stock and our profits are smaller. We, as individuals, don't have the same impact on a market that an institutional trader might have.

For instance, if a major financial institution suddenly offloads a high volume of stock then this will likely have a noticeable effect on the price of that stock. In this case, investors would see this as a warning sign and the value of the stock would go down. On the other hand, if a major financial institution suddenly acquires a huge amount of stock in a certain company, it may be a sign to investors and traders that they should buy this stock as well.

Financial institutions often have entire teams devoted to the research and analysis of certain stocks, which means retail traders often look to them as a source of information. If a large financial institution makes a move, then traders will assume that there is some meaning behind it.

Just because a financial institution can make these types of waves in the stock market does not mean that they are immune to the risks associated with trading and investing. As a matter of fact, in some cases the opposite is true. Because they have such an enormous number of stocks, it's more difficult for a financial institution to abandon a position when it starts to go south. The high volume also means that there is a higher risk; there is more money on the line. Think of the difference between a massive ship and a small fishing boat. The massive ship can carry more tuna, that's an indisputable fact. But if a storm is coming, the fishing boat can turn around in a hurry; whereas the ship needs more time to change its course.

Even though, as a retail trader, you'll be competing with these major financial institutions, you can take advantage of opportunities that they wouldn't be able to. You will be more flexible and more agile when the stock market changes its course. You'll be able to enter a position quickly when you see an opportunity or exit a position equally fast when things are moving against you. Institutional traders don't have that luxury.

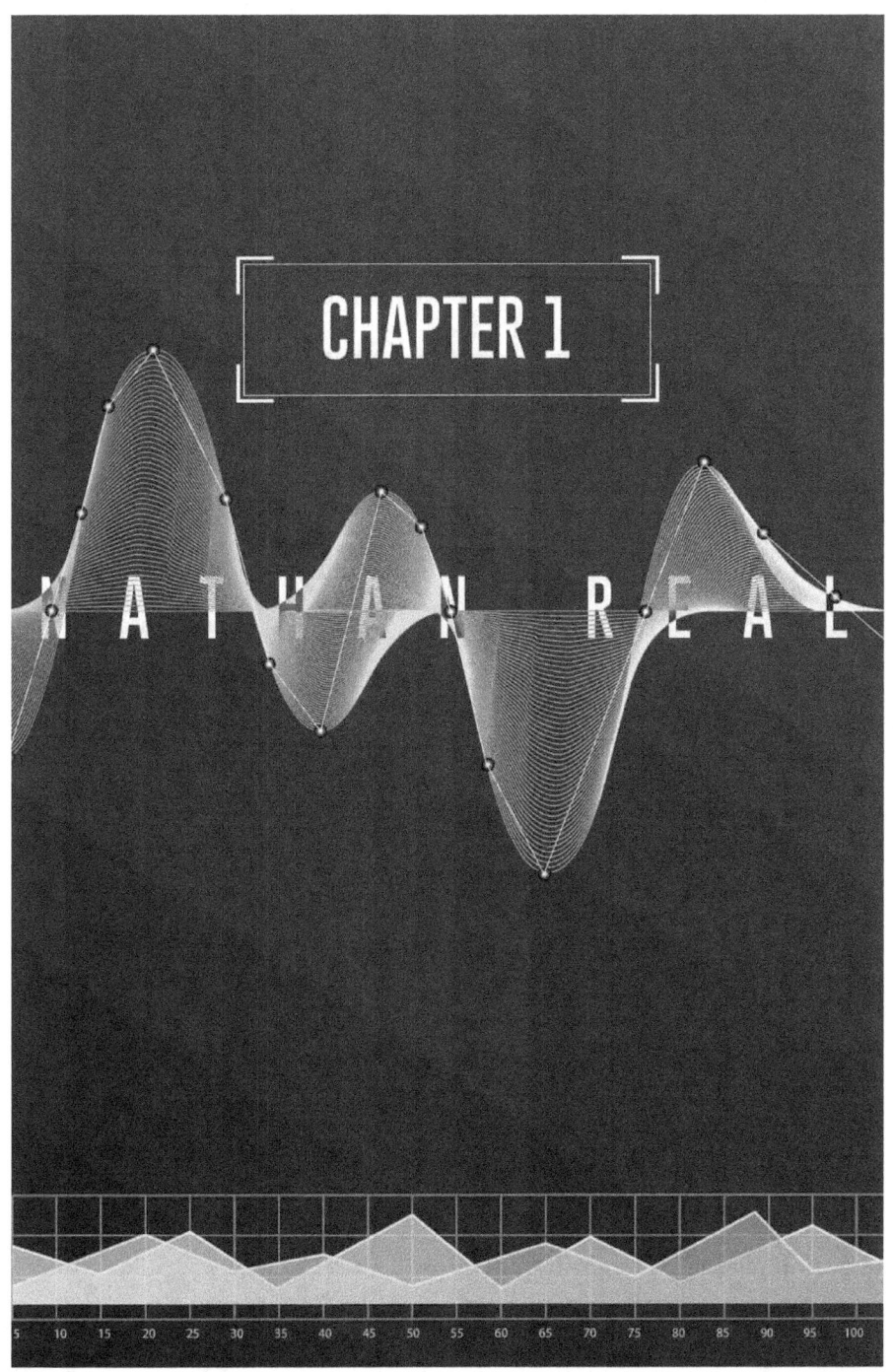

CHAPTER 1

NATHAN REAL

Chapter 1: What Kind of Trader Are You?

When people refer to retail, 'stay-at-home' traders they often call these people day traders. Retail traders can fall into many different categories depending on the type of strategy they employ. But what is the difference between a swing trader and a day trader? Is there a difference?

If you are a retail trader, then there are three categories that you could fall in to. Traders can either be classified as day traders, swing traders, or long-term position traders. You might even fall into more than one of these categories. You could use a mix of all three. The key difference is in the time frame of the position that these three types of traders will use. The three types of trades also require traders with different mindsets and strategies. They require a different degree of focus on the market, and some types of trades require a more active trader.

We talked earlier about the different types of trends, and how long they last. The trader who works with the shortest time frame is the day trader. The day trader looks to ride small, short term fluctuations that last less than a day. A day trader will be less focused on the overall trend in the market, and more focused on the small adjustments that happen throughout the market during a single given trading day. When the market opens, the day trader will have no positions from the day before. Instead, they will choose all new positions. By the time the trading day ends, the day trader will have exited all the positions they chose at the beginning of that day. Day traders can utilize short selling, options, and bullish techniques to make a profit. Day trading tends to lean heavily on technical analysis. A day trader might be less concerned with the actual company than with the patterns in the company's stock on a given day.

The downside of being a day trader is a time commitment. Most day traders use day trading as their main source of income; spending the entire day from market open until close watching movements in the stock market. You can't really be a passive day trader. In order to day trade successfully, you need to have enough time on your hands that you can monitor your positions minute by minute and make decisions as things unfold in the market.

Because the movements in day trading are typically small, the profits are also small. This means that a day trader relies on a high number of smaller successful trades. Hopefully, when you add up all your trades, you will have enough money to pay the bills. This means that a day trader must have a larger amount of starting capital in order to make the profits of day trading worth it. If you don't have a good amount of capital and a willingness to quit your day job, day trading isn't the most practical option.

In fact, I recommend that people shouldn't even consider day trading unless they have a healthy amount of experience in the stock market. Most people who attempt to become day traders will fail.

Sure, it is possible to make a lot of money very fast as a day trader. But that means its also possible to lose as much money, just as quickly. Day trading isn't a safe way to get rich, and its not a trading strategy for novice traders. It requires an in-depth understanding of the intricacies of the stock market, and the discipline to study and make high-stress decisions.

If you imagine day trading to be a laid back, work from home type of job, then you'd be mistaken. Day trading is a high-risk pursuit. Day traders must make decisions in a matter of minutes, or even seconds, about high volumes of their hard-earned money. The job does have its benefits; you can work from home and make your money independently of a boss. You don't have to commute to an office every day and you can take a day or two off without getting approval from HR first. These benefits are attached to a job that can be high risk, with a high degree of day traders burning out not long after their first trade.

But there is an alternative option. The risks and the rewards are slightly lower, as is the required investment of time and money. If you picked up this book, then you probably already know that day trading may not be the most feasible option for you as a trader. As a swing trader, you can still maintain a day job if you have access to a smartphone or a computer intermittently throughout the day. For a trader who is still learning the ropes, swing trading gives you more time to consider your positions which mean that the stress factor is slightly lower for a swing trader. Rather than being forced to make a guess on a position in a matter of a few minutes, swing traders can consider their next move over the course of a few hours or an entire day before they decide.

If you picked up this book, then you're interested in the second type of trading. Swing trading is like day trading; you're watching for short- and medium-term positions dependent on smaller adjustments in the overall trend. Swing traders have more time. The medium-term trends tend to move more which means that a swing trader will have the opportunity to profit more from one trade, but they will make fewer trades than the day trader. Slightly larger margins mean that a swing trader doesn't need quite as much capital when they initially invest.

If you want to trade actively, but you don't have the experience or the capital to trade full time, then swing trading is a good option. If you can monitor your portfolio from your phone or work computer, then you should be able to operate as a swing trader. The biggest factor in choosing what type of trader you want to come down to the lifestyle you want and skill level you possess.

The third type of trading that people employ is long term and position investing. While this type of trading doesn't really fit within the scope of this book, many swing traders and day traders will choose to hold these types of positions in order to diversify their strategies. A position investor will plan to hold on to a stock for a significant period; choosing a stock that they think is undervalued or has the potential for growth in the future. Fundamental analysis is the most important thing to a position investor. If you are interested in a company over a long period of time, then you will analyze the fundamentals of stock before deciding to invest. A position investor will probably expect to hold their position for years, using their investment as more of a savings tool than an active trading tool.

Position investing is considered the lowest risk form of investing. If you have a well-diversified investment portfolio then the average of all your stocks should go up over time. If you hold onto those investments through all the dips and peaks, then your initial investment will hopefully have grown.

The most important consideration for choosing which type of time frame strategy you want to use will be dependent on your personality. What is your temperament and ability to handle stress, and how much time do you have to commit to trading?

There is nothing wrong with choosing the lower risk route of position investing with the occasional swing trade. In fact, most retail investors and traders fall within this category. For many people, this is the right place to be. If you are more risk-averse, then the stock market may serve better as a savings tool than as an active source of income.

There is a whole spectrum of trading that you can take part in, from position investing to day trading. The trick is to find the strategies and the level of participation that suits your life and your willingness to take risks. If you figure out what type of strategies suit you then you will be more likely to stick with trading and less likely to suffer from the burnout that is common among new traders who bite off more than they can chew. It's not a bad idea to start trading with simpler strategies and slowly move towards more active types of trading. Most experienced traders will have a portfolio that contains a mix of different types of investments with different time-oriented strategies. You can be a swing trader and a day trader and a position investor all at once. Just make sure you know what you're doing so that you don't overwhelm yourself.

There is also a difference in the amount of capital required to begin trading with any of these strategies. Day traders require the most amount of capital to begin. Most day trading accounts require a minimum investment of $25,000. This is not a small amount of money, and more than most beginner investors are willing to use. They require more money because their margins are smaller.

Swing traders require less. You can start a swing trading account with as little as $5000. It would be difficult to swing trade with any amount of capital much lower than that. Some people manage to swing trade with accounts that are as small as $1000, but this makes it difficult to diversify. If you're a long-term position investor, then there is really no minimum threshold. However, the same problems exist for long term investors; with less money, it will be more difficult to diversify, especially if you are managing your portfolio independently.

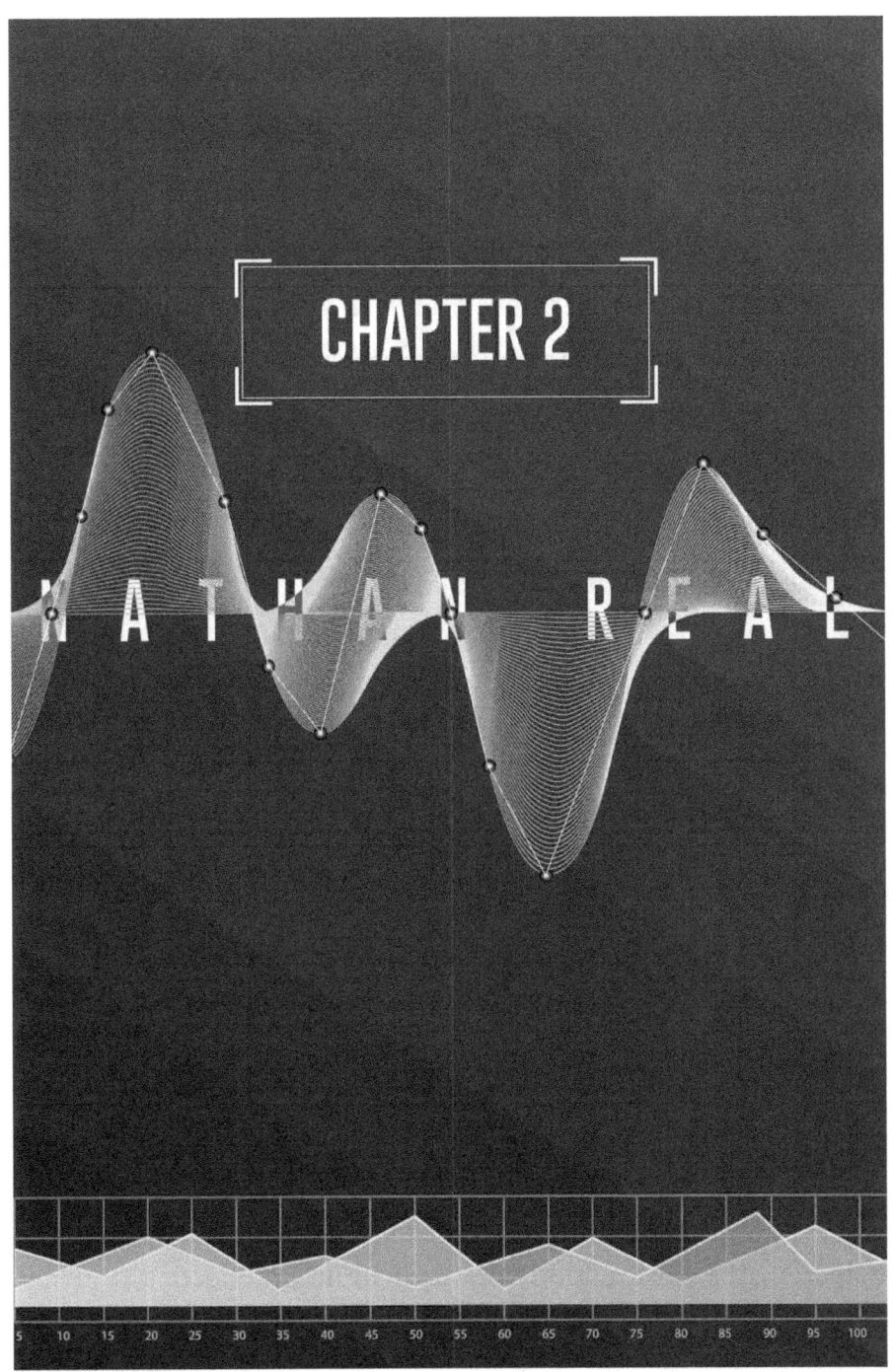

CHAPTER 2

Chapter 2: How to Buy and Sell Stocks

In order to buy and sell stocks, we must go through someone called a broker. A broker's job is to connect buyers and sellers on the stock market. If you've ever seen videos or pictures of the New York Stock Exchange, you've likely seen brokers moving around between the screens talking on the phone and brokering deals between traders.

You and I can't go to the New York Stock Exchange and start buying and selling shares independently. We must go through a licensed brokerage. With the advent of the internet, the cost of finding a brokerage has gone down and there are more options available that are more attractive to smaller retail traders. This has opened the door to new strategies and has made retail trading more accessible to anyone with a computer and internet access.

It doesn't take a large amount of money or an expensive broker to make some money on the stock market nowadays. The only requirements are the willingness to take on some degree of risk and the ability to read a few different types of charts. A good predilection to market research and financial analysis will also help. All the information you need to be an effective trader is available through your phone or home computer.

There are many different types of brokerages available through the internet, where you can manage your portfolio and make trades in one place. The type of brokerage you choose will depend on the amount of money you're investing as well. We'll talk about this later on in the book, but choosing a brokerage is the first step in trading or investing and it requires some thought and research once you've learned a little more about the different types of trading strategies and what sort of features you consider to be the most important.

When you are looking to buy a stock, you will see two different prices. The first price is called the asking price. It's a little like the 'buy it now price'. As an alternative, you can also buy a stock at the bid price. The bid price will be lower than the asking price which means you can get a better deal on the stock if the broker is willing to part with the stock at that price. Just like any time you make a deal, whether on the stock market or at a garage sale, offering a lower price means that there is a chance you may not get the stock you're bidding for. This means that if you're trying to quickly enter the market in order to capitalize on a trend, you might miss out if you bid and don't get the stock.

Whether a not a broker will sell you the stock for the bid price is dependent on many factors. The stock market is an experiment in the laws of supply in demand which means that a broker will make his or her decision based on these laws. If the stock is in low demand, you may be able to buy it for a price much lower than the asking price. If not, many people are buying the stock then the broker will be much more willing to part with it for a low price.

On the other hand, if the market indicators show that a stock is quickly on the rise and traders are seeing an opportunity forming, then the demand for that stock is probably going to increase. If you offer the broker a bid that's too low, then he'll probably turn it down because he can find someone to pay more for the stock.

Keep this in mind when you are going to purchase a stock. You might be able to save some money by buying a stock below the asking price. But if you have a feeling that the stock is in high demand, don't try and low-ball the broker because they will probably find a more willing buyer and you will lose the stock altogether and miss out on whatever trend you're following.

As traders, we can trade with two different kinds of accounts. When you sign up with a broker you will have the option of choosing one or the other. Most brokerages will give you a choice between the two. For many new traders, they open their account and are asked whether they want to open a cash account, or a margin account and they don't know the difference.

The main difference between a cash account and a margin account is the way they allow you to use your available funds. If you went to a bank and asked to get a card, you'd be given the choice between a debit card and a credit card. If you choose to get a debit card, then the card acts much like a regular wallet. You can only spend the money that you have in your wallet, you can't spend money you don't have on hand. If you choose to get a credit card then you have the option to purchase things, pay the bank back later. When the brokerage gives you the choice between a cash account and a margin account, your options are similar.

If you open a cash account and deposit $10,000 dollars, it means that you can buy $10,000 dollars' worth of stock. It's like a debit card. You can buy as much stock as you want, splitting your account however you want, by purchasing the stock with the cash available in your account.

This is the most straightforward way of managing your money whether you are getting a bank card or opening a brokerage account. However, there is a reason that people decide to get credit cards. With a credit card, you have more flexibility. If you have a bill to pay now, but your paycheck comes next week then you're able to pay the bill and cover it later.

By opening a margin account, you receive flexibility from the broker, who is extending credit to you so that you can buy stocks and pay later. If you open a margin account with $10,000 dollars, you can use the broker's credit to purchase stocks while the $10,000 acts as leverage for the credit.

Let's say that your $10,000 is tied up in stocks that you can't sell at the moment, but an opportunity has popped up that you want to take a position on. You don't have the cash on hand immediately, but you know that in a few days you'll have the cash so you can pay the broker back at that time. The added flexibility of a margin account means you can take advantage of opportunities even when you don't have cash on hand.

The flipside of the margin account, just like with a credit card, is the added risk of borrowing money with the intention of paying it back later. If you leverage your $10,000 to purchase more stocks on credit, then those stocks go down in prices then your losses are more than if you had just purchased the stock in cash. You'll lose on the stock dropping in price, but you'll still need to pay the broker back for the full price. Your broker might also get nervous that you won't pay them back. The broker might make you sell those stocks you have as leverage, and if you are selling them at a bad time then your losses will be even worse. You'll lose not only the money from the bad trade, but you'll lose the stock and the potential earnings from the shares you purchased in cash.

If you want to minimize risk as much as possible, then the best choice is to choose a cash account. This is often a good idea for newer investors. But if you avoid the risk by choosing a cash account then you will also lose out on the added benefits of using a margin account. Some swing trading strategies require a margin account, so you'll be unable to apply these strategies. There are ways to maintain a credit card in a safe and conservative manner, while still enjoying the benefits of having credit. Margin accounts can also be used safely if you minimize the amount of leverage you use and limiting your use of credit to certain scenarios.

Before choosing between a margin and a cash account, make sure you read the terms that apply to your brokerage. Many brokerages have rules for how much you can leverage and minimum amounts for opening a margin account. Once you've finished reading the rest of this book you will have a better idea of what types of strategies you want to use, and which account will be the most suitable. If you want to keep your trading simple and minimize risk when you are first starting out, then consider opening a cash account. But keep in mind the added flexibility and the ability to capitalize on opportunities when you don't have the cash immediately available. A higher potential for profits always comes with added risk, and vice versa.

Once you've opened your account, you'll start to watch the market, maybe even picking a few specific stocks to watch. You're watching in order to choose a good position. When traders refer to a position, they are talking about the stocks that they decide to buy or short in anticipation of the stock moving up or down. The most basic example of a position is buying a stock anticipating that the price will go up in the future so that you can sell it at a higher price.

While it may seem obvious that people make money on the stock market when the prices go up, there also traders whose strategies depend on the stock market going down by using a method called shorting. It's a higher risk strategy that is quite common among day traders and swing traders.

Short selling works like this; a trader has a gut feeling that the price of a stock will drop soon. They've seen the indicators and they think the stock is overvalued for whatever reason, and they anticipate a decline in the price followed by a high volume of traders offloading the stock at the same. But how can a trader profit off this scenario?In this instance, the trader doesn't own any of this stock. So, in order to short sell, he or she borrows shares of that company from the broker and then sells them.

Remember that this trader anticipated a drop in the price of this stock. Now that they've sold it, they wait. Eventually they will have to pay back the broker for the borrowed stock. If they were right about the stock price plummeting, then by the time they pay their broker back for the shorted stock they will only have to pay back a fraction of what they bought the stock for. They make their profit in the beginning by selling high and buying low, rather than the ordinary trade which happens in the reverse.

The risk with short selling, of course, is that the price of the stock might go up instead of down. It might turn out that the gut feeling you had about a stock being undervalued was wrong; instead of the price plummeting as you expected, it just keeps going up.No matter how high it goes, you will have to buy the stock back for your broker. If I short $200 worth of shares hoping that tomorrow they will go down, but instead they are suddenly worth $300 this means that I'll have lost $100. You might consider waiting, maybe you mistimed the drop, but the shares might still go down. You wait a few days and now the stocks you shorted are valued at $400. So, you received $200 from short selling, but you owe your broker $400. The dangerous thing about short selling is that you have no idea how high a stock price can go up. If the stock is overvalued and the price has been rising, then there is a chance that it could continue doing that and it may not stop in foreseeable future.

With short selling, it's a lot trickier to turn the boat around and minimize your losses.

The advantage of short selling is that when you rely on the stock price going up to make money, you usually must wait much longer to see the price rise. When the price of a stock rises, it usually increases slowly over time which means that someone anticipating a stock price increase must wait longer to see the same profits as a short seller. When the price of a stock drops, it drops quickly due to market psychology. You can make a quick profit with short selling.

Some people question short selling, saying that it poses a moral hazard. Profiting off a market that is going down, or a business that is doing poorly. The questionable ethics of short selling have led to regulation of short selling which means restrictions on the times that traders can short stocks. For example, you can short sell in a market that's already in recession. The market has been moving upward for a trader to engage in short selling.

In the early days of the stock market, people who try to make money by instigating a price drop. A large group would short sell a stock at the same time. A high volume of short-sellers at once would cause the market to panic and people would start to sell their own shares creating an artificial drop in price.

Proponents of short selling argue that they are doing the stock market a favor. They are helping to predict downturns and warn the public about overvalued stocks. In 2008, short-sellers made billions of dollars by anticipating the collapse of the housing market, short selling a large volume of stocks right before the Great Recession.

Short selling is an important tool because it gives us a method of profiting in all kinds of situations. You don't need to wait for a stock to go up in price in order to make money. You can make money off a stock whose price is going up; known as a bullish stock. You can also make money short selling on a bearish stock. The bull and the bear are classic wall street symbols for the different types of market trends. A bull market is named after the way a bull attack by thrusting its horns up, so a bull market is moving up. The bear market gets its name from the downwards swipe of a bear's claws when it attacks. Financial analysts often refer to stocks being bullish and bearish, while the market might be a bull market or a bear market.

For a market or a stock to qualify as being bearish, then we need to see a downward trend over a given a trend over a period. Not every downward movement in the price of a stock makes the stock bearish. If analysts start referring to a bear market, the stock market would have to have experienced a loss of 20% or more of its overall value. A bear market must occur over an extended period. In 2008, when the stock market experienced a great recession, stocks were bearish for over 17 months.

A bear market is often, but not always, correlated with an economy that is not doing well. When growth starts to slow down in the market, investors begin to feel less confident about the economy. After all, what goes up must always down? Investors see the slowing growth and anticipate a drop. They'll either start investing less or selling off investments to protect themselves from the drop that they anticipate.

When a significant number of investors begin to act this way then the demand for stocks will go down, which means the price of the stocks will go down and the drop will be exacerbated by the collective panic. Many investors begin to fear a bear market when the prices for stocks are peaking but the outlook for the companies, they are investing in begins to drop. The market will remain bearish until investors anticipate it to turn around again.

A bull market happens when the value of the market is increasing over time. Not every increase in the market is bullish, but like bear markets, the market value needs to be increasing for a good amount of time for it to qualify as a true bull market. When the market is bullish, investors will see this as an opportunity. They expect the prices will continue to rise, so they buy stock in order to make some money from the increase.

So, with swing traders buying and selling a stock, they have an opportunity to make money off of the market in a variety of conditions. The simplest approach is buying low and selling high. Making money on a bullish market is less risky, and the most straightforward. It's also the way an investor will make their money if they are waiting for a profit from a long-term investment. If you want to make money on a bullish market, then the best time to buy a stock is often during a bearish market. If you use this approach, you will have to be willing to wait for however long it's necessary for the market to turn around and move upwards again.

The short-selling stock has the potential for quick profits, but they come with higher risk. Short selling is one of the most common methods of swing trading. Unlike buying stock and hoping for a bullish market, short selling requires less patience because the time frame is shorter. You must be aware though, that this means you can lose a lot more in a shorter amount of time. Short selling is a more active swing trading strategy that requires an astute trader who is willing to keep up with market trends as they unfold.

Keep in mind that some brokerage companies, especially for small-time traders, don't offer short selling. For example,

Robinhood is a popular app for many beginning investors because it has no trading fees which mean that you can trade with even a small amount of money without your profits being eaten away by fees.

This brings us to our next section where we will discuss the different types of swing trading. Knowing a little bit about these strategies will help you choose a broker. You can identify which brokers have these tools available. An important factor to consider is the fees that the broker will charge. Depending on the amount of money you are trading with, these fees will quickly add up if you're making multiple trades. If you're only using a small amount of money, then you'll spend more money on fees than you'll be profiting. Therefore, it's important to think about the strategy you want to use when you're swing trading before you choose a broker. Different brokers will come with different features and will enable different strategies. The amount of money you start with will also be an important consideration.

Once you've chosen your broker, you will have to decide which type of account is best for you. Whether that's a margin account or a cash account, you will have different advantages depending on the one you choose. Of course, your skill level and your level of experience should be an important factor when you're considering a broker. A margin account might give you more flexibility and might make it possible to achieve higher profits, but the risk will be higher. How much do you want to risk when you are first starting out? There are a lot of things to watch for when you're trading stock; sometimes the best solution is keeping your trades simple when you're first starting out.

We mentioned Robinhood as a popular choice for beginning investors. You can trade with a smaller amount of money because there are no commissions for trades. The biggest downside to using Robinhood is the fact that they don't allow you to short. If you are a beginning investor only interested in trading bullishly, then this won't be a problem. If you're a more experienced investor and you want to tap into the profits from short selling and use strategies that only work on a bearish market, then opening an account with Robinhood will be limiting. There's nothing wrong in starting with simple strategies and smaller amounts of capital. For this, there is nothing wrong with choosing a service like Robinhood while you learn the ropes and do your first trades. You'll save money on commission fees and you will have a relatively simple setup to begin trading. You might read this book and think you've got a pretty good grasp on swing trading and jump right into using multiple strategies on a complex platform. The truth is, once the ticker starts moving and you must make decisions, a lot of the information you retained will be lost in the heat of the moment.

Remember, there is nothing wrong with starting out using simple strategies.

You'll also want to think about what the brokerage platforms will provide in terms of technical assistance. Most decent trading apps will give you the ability to monitor your portfolio in real-time, but there are added features that can be helpful when you start using more comprehensive strategies. In order to streamline the process, buying and selling stocks should be as easy as possible through your brokerage account.

In addition to that actual trading of stocks through your broker, many apps offer a comprehensive analysis in real-time. Many apps also offer the added benefit of access to market research and in-depth coverage of certain stocks. This by itself shouldn't be the only selling point. Most of the research provided can be found on your own. If you want to have the research available in one place, then using an app that provides this will be useful but not totally necessary.

What is more useful is finding brokerage fees that can send you text and email alerts about a stock movement. If you're a swing trader then you probably aren't monitoring the market during every minute that it's open, but you should be able to keep close tabs on it especially if you are anticipating a movement. If you are waiting to decide on a position, your brokerage can send you text alerts when the price of a stock goes up or below a certain alert price. This enables you to keep track of your stocks or potential opportunities even while you busy at work or running errands. You never know when an opportunity may present itself.

Stock Options

Another way to add flexibility to your trading strategy is by using stock options. Stock options are especially popular in recent years because they can be an effective way of lowering risk while also giving you the ability to hedge several positions at once without tying up your capital until you know you want to make a move.

Options consist of puts and calls. When you buy a stock option, you are paying a broker to hold a stock a certain price for you. Let's say a new kid moves into the neighborhood, he has a trading card that you think is worth a lot of money. You want to wait to buy it, but you think that other kids in the neighborhood will want it as well. You tell the new kid that you think that trading card is worth $7, and you offer him $2 to hold the price at $7. The next day, the rest of the kids in the neighborhood see the trading card and offer him $10 for it. But you've already made a deal, paying him $2 to hold on to the card for you at a fixed price. You buy the card for the fixed price you've agreed upon, and then turn around and sell it to the kids offering $10. This is essentially how an option works.

When you buy a stock option, you are purchasing the option to buy it and sell it at a higher price later down the road. Let's say instead that you give your neighbor $2 to hold the price at $7 for you. Tomorrow the kids in the neighborhood show up, but they don't think the card is as valuable as you do. They only offer him $5. You decide in that case, not to buy the card from him at $7, because it's not worth as much as you thought. Instead of being out $7, you are only out $2 because you didn't purchase the card outright. You just paid the cardholder to hold it for you at a certain price.

With stock options, you're paying the broker to hold it at a fixed price. If you see a stock that you think might go up, you can buy an option from the broker to hold it at the current price. If the stock goes up, then you will make a profit because the broker will still sell it to you at the discounted price. If it goes down, then you'll only lose the option fee rather than the entire price of purchasing the stock. Stock options allow you to set a price for yourself without committing the amount of capital it would take to buy the stock outright.

The fee that you pay the broker to hold the stock at a price is known as a strike price. In options trading, if the stock doesn't do as well as you'd hoped then ideally you will only lose the strike price rather than the entire price of the stock. If your broker is sitting on a stock valued at $15, you can pay them $3 in order to hold the stock at that price. If the value of that stock goes up to $22 next week, then you pay your broker $15 and then sell the stock. Your call on this option will have made you a $4 profit. What if, however, you pay your broker $3 to hold the stock at $15. Next week the price of the stock drops to $10. If you had bought the stock outright then you would have lost $5. By buying an option on this stock, you instead will only lose the $3 you paid for the strike price.

Typically, options have expiration dates. You can't buy an option and hold onto it indefinitely; the broker will set a day and you must choose to exercise the option by that day. Brokers will usually sell options in sets, with 100 shares per set. It allows you to gain an advantage in several opportunities, without committing to the risk of tying up too much capital. Trading options are a way to keep your portfolio flexible and react to the market, rather than being fixed to a position. It's a way to make your portfolio more diverse even when you are working with a smaller amount of money.

There are major advantages to shifting your strategy towards trading options. On the flip side, they are also more complicated than normal trades. It requires a good amount of organization to manage your options, which is usually done the best when you have some experience as a trader. When you own a stock, then you know what price you bought it for and what you stand to gain or lose at any given time. When you own stocks, there isn't any confusion when you look over your portfolio. If you trade options you will have to pay closer attention to your buy and sell price, as well as your strike price. You must not only sell for a profit but sell for a profit that is large enough to cover the cost of your strike price. Choosing to use an option and selling a stock too early can result in a negative result, even when the trade was positive. It's an easy mistake to make when you are first learning how to trade options.

Another advantage of option trading is the number of opportunities at any given time. Options traders can be flexible where regular bull and bear traders become fixed in a position once they've entered it. For beginner traders, I recommend spending some time using simpler strategies before you start to try options trading. While options trading has an added degree of flexibility, it is much more complicated. There are entire books devoted to different options trading strategies, with strategies much more involved than swing trading strategies. Its good to understand what's out there in terms of potential strategies, so you can plan and choose a broker that will enable you to use these strategies in the future. Like any type of trading, options traders need to be diligent and focused in order to be successful. Passive beginner traders should probably shy away from options trading when they first start.

Exchange Traded Funds

Another way for small-time retail traders to diversify their portfolio is by using exchange traded funds. If you are a beginner and you don't have a lot of initial capital, then exchange traded funds are a good way to stretch your money to create a more diverse array of investments. They are easy to buy and sell and they don't require a large degree of capital to invest in, so they are simple to use and a good way to learn the stock market.

The diversity of exchange traded funds is their main advantage. The spread between the bid and ask price is typically lower so buying and selling are straightforward. Exchange traded funds are a combined list of stocks within a given sector. If you were smart, then you'd choose a sector where you already have a good amount of knowledge. That way you'll know what pieces of information to watch for. Having some technical knowledge about the companies you own share in gives you an advantage because when you are doing market research or research on specific companies, you might notice things that someone else would overlook. Just like if you were to buy a business, you would have more success if you bought a business where you understood the product and the relevant market. You'd know what companies to watch for and what new technologies might cause a change in the market. I recommend that as a beginning investor you pick ETFs in a sector that already interests you, where you won't mind doing research.

Diversification is one of the most important ways to minimize risk. The value of some stocks may drop, but overall the value of a well-diversified portfolio is more likely to go up. If you want to diversify your portfolio as a new swing trader, then this is the cheapest way to do it. ETFs can also be traded using the strategies we've already mentioned, such as short selling and options trading. It's worth reading up on exchange traded funds if you are a new investor and you want to add a little more horsepower to your trading strategies.

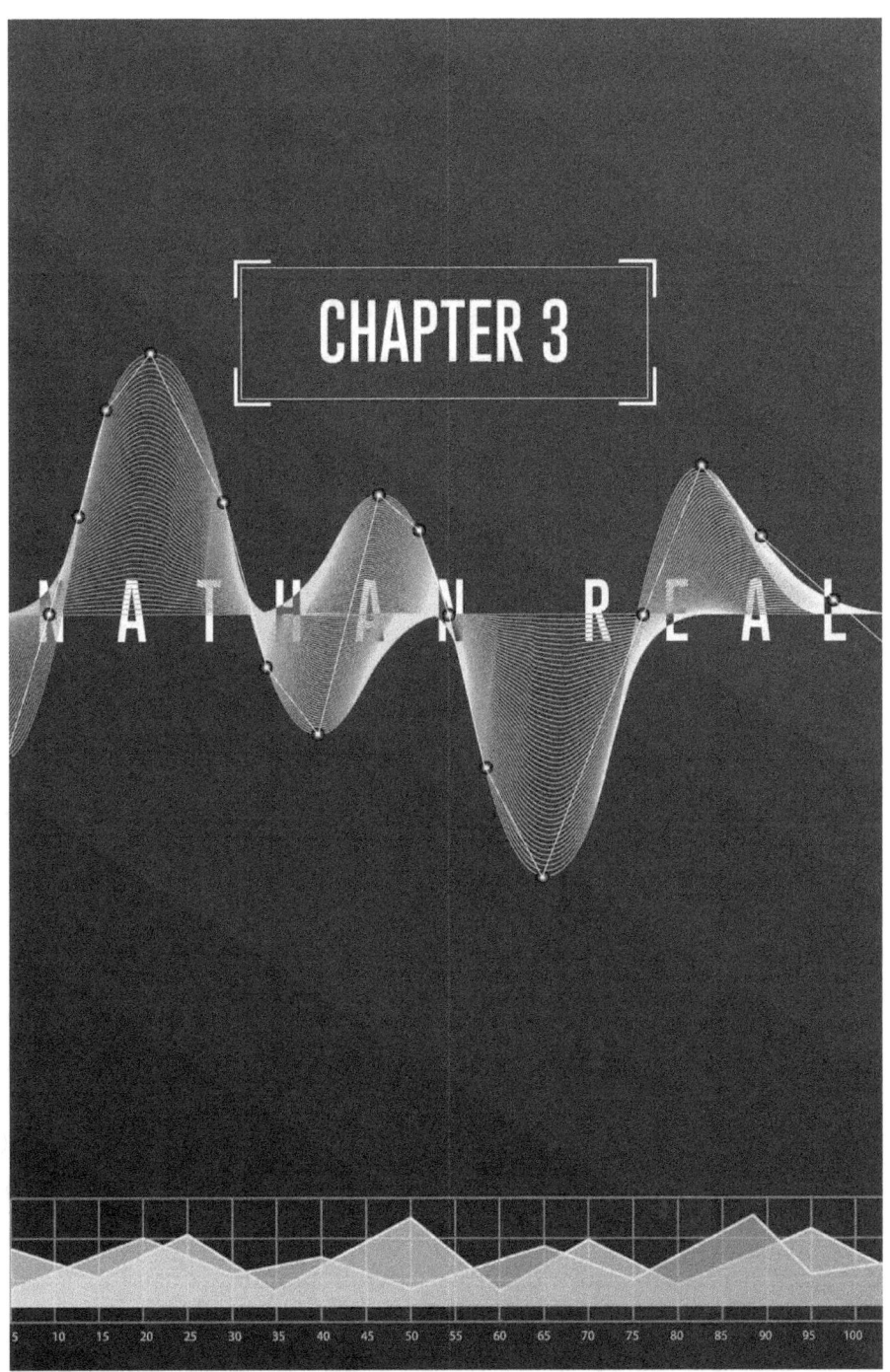

CHAPTER 3

NATHAN REAL

Chapter 3: How to Read the Market

By now we have talked about a few different types of trades that a swing trader can use. All these types of trades, whether you are using short selling or options or buying bullish stocks, require you to examine market factors to determine where you are most likely to make a profit. But there are thousands of stocks available on the market which you could take a position with for swing trading, so how do you know which stocks are worth watching? What types of indicators do successful traders look for?

In this chapter, we focus on the tools used by traders and investors to study the value of a stock and to make predictions about our expectations. As traders, we use two different types of analysis to make predictions or guesses about the projected value of a stock. The first type of analysis is called fundamental analysis and when we do fundamental analysis, we are looking at the actual business indicators relevant to stock, like the way we would evaluate the health of a business we were going to buy.

The second type of analysis is called technical analysis. When you look at a financial website like Finviz, you will see dozens of different numbers and indicators as well as numerous charts, all tracking different parts of the stock market. We call these technical indicators. Traders look for patterns and trends in technical indicators to make predictions.

Fundamental Analysis

Fundamental analysis is a way for traders to get insight into the performance of a business over time. Recall that we compared buying stock to buying an actual business. If I wanted to purchase a brick and mortar store, I'd be interested in looking at the numbers of how the business is performing. Fundamental analysis is very similar to the type of analysis you would do if you wanted to buy a business. You'd probably want to know things like how much profit the business is making, or how much debt the business has.

These indicators would give you a good picture of how the business is performing so that you could make a prediction about its long-term prospects. Is common sense that buying an unprofitable business would be a higher risk than buying a business that was doing very well? But it follows that the profitable business would be much more expensive to buy. We use fundamental indicators to determine whether the price of the stock matches what we think the stock is worth based on our fundamental analysis.

If we wanted to know the profits that a business is making, then we want to know the profit that a stock will get us. The first fundamental analysis measurement is called **earnings per share.** When we buy a stock or a share in a business, we are only buying a small percentage of that business. With earnings per share, we are calculating how much of the profit we will get for our own in the company. You can find the earnings per share of a company by taking the profit of a company and dividing it by the number of shares that a company has issued. The better the earnings per share are, the higher the value it is given by the market. A stock with high earnings per share is seen as valuable because people expect the company to continue to make profits.

The next thing you would want to know about a business you are buying would be the prospects for earning in the future. A company that is profitable today still needs to innovate and compete in the market so that it can continue to be profitable tomorrow.

If you wanted to see how business was growing, you would look at its growth over time. Has growth been stagnant? Has there been a decline in growth over the past few years? By looking at growth over time, you might have an idea of what the prospects look like for the company. Traders and investors use what's called projected earnings growth to determine the prospects for growth of a company so that they can find the value of the company. To find the projected earnings growth you would divide the price of the stock by its earnings per share, and then divide that value by the growth of earnings per share.

Not every analyst will use the exact same formula for calculating projected earnings growth. While this information is typically free to access companies' earnings reports, different companies may use slightly different methods of calculating projected earnings growth. Keep this in mind when you are looking at projected earnings growth so that your comparisons are made using consistent data.

Projected earnings growth is a useful tool when combined with earnings per share. Of course, if you see high earnings per share but a low price for the stock, you might think you are getting a good deal. If you take a closer look and see that the projected earnings growth is low or declining, then that might explain the reason why the stock is discounted.

While you might think you are getting a good deal based on earnings per share, the project earnings growth is a good tool to double-check and evaluate whether the prospects are good for the company and whether that high earnings per share will continue.

The same applies to stock with the opposite fundamentals. Maybe you see a stock that has low earnings per share, or the price for the stock seems too high relative to the earnings that you'll receive. Based on these fundamentals you might conclude that the stock is overvalued. However, a high projected earnings growth might give you enough reason to suspect that the prospects for the company look very good, even if their actual earnings per share are low now. After all, if you are long term investment then you will be looking for companies that will grow over time. You could argue the projected growth earnings are equally important as earnings per share for a long-term investor.

A company can evaluate the value of its own stock, which might be different from what the market will pay. This is known as the price equity ratio. A company uses its own fundamentals to determine the value of its stock and then compares it to the value given by the market. Using this ratio can help you determine if a company is undervalued or overvalued. A company with a high price equity ratio may be overvalued, while a company with a low-price equity ratio might be undervalued.

Another way to earn money through owning stocks is in dividends. Dividends are returns paid by the company for the shares of that company which you own. It's like the company giving you a small piece of their profits in return for owning some stock. Some people choose to reinvest their dividends in order to extend their ownership of a company. Not all the company's income is paid out in dividends though. A good percentage of the money earned by a company goes back into the company to pay expenses and grow. Another fundamental that traders can look for in a company is the dividend payout ratio. This amount of income that goes back to the shareholders, relative to the total income with the dividend payout ratio you are basically finding out; how big of a cut am I getting, relative to the entire pie?

Some companies will have higher dividend payout ratios, so this is another type of fundamental. Obviously the higher the price, the higher you would hope to get in return for the dividend payout. If you want to know how much you are making in dividends relative to the price you are paying for the stock, you would look at the **dividend yield**. You can use the dividend to compare the amount you will get in dividends relative to the price, and then compare this across companies. If the dividend yield is low compared to stocks at similar prices, then this is a negative indicator.

Companies need to own assets in order to function. Assets can be anything from machinery to materials, to intellectual property. Assets cost money, which means that the return on these assets is important to shareholders. You want to know that the assets are not only being paid for but that they are paying for themselves. If a company has a lot of assets, but their income is low relative to these assets, then this might be a red flag as a potential investor. The company is spending a lot of money on these assets, but the returns aren't that impressive relative to what the company has invested. The fundamental used to determine this is known as return on equity. To find equity, take the cost of the assets less the debt incurred to buy those assets. Then divide the company's income by that number. This will provide you with a return on equity.

Keep in mind that what is considered 'good' return on equity will depend on the industry. Different industries will require different assets, so the cost of operating the business and the margins will be slightly different. The overhead costs in one industry will be completely different from one type of company to the next.

An airline may have very expensive assets with smaller margins than an insurance company. Don't confuse yourself by comparing the return on equity of two companies in totally different sectors, because the comparison won't mean much. Instead, compare the return on equity for similar companies. If you are looking at buying stocks in Northwest Airlines, compare their return on equity to that of Lufthansa. Then you can compare the efficiency of two companies that provide the same service which requires similar assets.

On the other side of equity, a company also will manage some level of debt. While debt may seem like a dirty word to the individual, it is a tool that corporate managers can use to leverage their capital in order to grow and expand. Companies will take on debt in order to buy equipment or hire specialists to design a new product line. It's not unusual for companies to have some amount of debt for a variety of reasons. If a company manages its debt effectively, then they can drive expansion.

If you were going to buy a business, you would want to know if that business was in debt and why. You'd also probably ask if the company had an effective plan to pay off the debt. How much debt does the business have, relative to its assets and earnings? If we are planning to trade, we would ask the same question about a company whose stock we considered taking a position on. In order to make an assessment on a company's debt management, we would look at the fundamental known as the debt to equity ratio.

How much does the company owner in assets, and how much are those assets worth? What is the ratio of this equity to the level of debt the company has taken on? The debt to equity ratio will help us answer these types of questions. For the most part, it's a good sign if a company has less debt than equity.

The next fundamental and the one that brings us back to our first point will help us determine whether the company is profitable or not. If I want to buy a bike shop, the obvious questions would be; how many bikes do you sell per month or per year? How much money do you make on repairs? Now apply those questions to a stock purchase. How much product has the company sold, be it goods or services? Multiply this by the value of all these goods or service, and you will end up with total revenue.In short, you're looking at how much money the company is taking in. Ideally, you'll be looking for a company whose total revenue is steadily increasing if you're interested in a long-term investment. Conversely, if a company has shown a steady decline then the stock price will also decline.

Why is Fundamental Analysis Important

To summarize; if you're a swing trader then you should take an interest in fundamental analysis. Knowing the health of a company that you want to buy a share of is the first step to investing and trading intelligently. Just like buying a business, you would want to know how that business is doing, and how it will do in the future.

With the accessibility of the internet, these fundamental indicators should be easy to find. Publicly traded companies should have earnings reports, investor reports, or financial reports which are tailored towards prospective investors doing research on the health of their company. While at first, it might seem daunting to look through these extensive reports, it is invaluable to you as a trader. Now that you understand which fundamentals to look for, you narrow the scope of your research and study important indicators more efficiently.

Fundamental analysis is also helpful because you will be able to compare the health of companies within the same sector. When you limit your research to a sector then the fundamentals will have appropriate context. With fundamental analysis, you are acknowledging that the price of the stock does not tell the entire story on its own. Look at the health indicators of a company, as well as the macroeconomic influences. The see how other companies are performing in the same circumstances. Try and give yourself a complete picture of the business before you decide to buy stock in the company. At the end of the day, treat it as if you are buying the entire business. What sort of questions would you ask the previous owners before risking your hard-earned capital?

Technical Analysis

We mentioned earlier that there are two different types of analysis that swing traders apply when they are trying to evaluate potential positions. Now, you have learned how to research the performance of a company, and how its internal indicators can influence your decisions on trading. That is the basis for fundamental analysis.

The second type of analysis is called technical analysis, and it involves the study of patterns in order to make decisions about trading positions. Technical analysists use historical data and statistics to examine patterns in the stock market. While these patterns may have variations, there are some patterns which are consistent and knowing how to recognize characteristics of these patterns will enable you to anticipate movements and make judgments about the psychology of the market.

While you are anticipating movements in the market and trying to determine your own positions, there are millions of other traders trying to do the same thing. Around the world, many of these traders are watching the candlestick charts and trying to make the same predictions that you are trying to make. All these traders are competing with the same thought in mind; making a profit.

Market psychology is important because sometimes the stock market anticipating a movement can become a self-fulfilling prophecy. If thousands of shareholders think that a stock price will plummet and they decide to sell off their stocks in a mass exodus, then the price of that stock will plummet. As a swing trader, you are trying to profit off short-term movements in the market. These short-term movements are often caused or exacerbated by the collective hive mind of traders anticipating the same thing. So, it is important for a swing trader to be able to use technical indicators to give them a clear picture of how other people are trading.

Technical analysis is dependent on economic theories and theories about the stock market that analysts have developed over time after studying the historic movements of the market. While fundamental analysis gives you a snapshot of a company and some indicators of long-term health, technical analysis is a more direct approach to try and predict stock prices using statistics.

Much of the market depends on the laws of supply and demand. Supply and demand will ultimately be the determinants of the market price of a stock. The more people want a stock, the higher the demand is. The demand for a stock will decrease when the price that stock increases. The more people are willing to pay for something, the higher the supply will go. Supply and demand interact with each other in markets until they reach a level of equilibrium. The price of the stock will sit at this equilibrium point.

On the stock market, the price of a stock is determined by the market factors affecting supply and demand. Many trade theorists believe that the price of stock accounts for all the factors in the market, which means that the price of a stock always reflects the true value of that stock determined by supply and demand. Trade theorists who follow this school of thought believe that the price is the only real indicator of all these elements combined. This is a belief held by many technical analysts.

The belief that the price of a stock is the best indicator of the market is a key component Dow Theory. If you follow the stock market, then the name Dow should be very familiar to you. The Dow Jones Industrial Average is a major index in the modern stock market.

It was named after Charles Dow, the founder of the Wall Street Journal and the architect for many modern theories of the stock market that are now important tenets for technical analysis. The Wall Street Journal started as a two-page pamphlet for investors in the 1870s but was eventually transformed into a full-fledged newspaper.

Charles Dow was an early component of the idea that the price of a stock reflected all the supply and demand factors in the market, and the market was always at the efficient equilibrium based on current market characteristics. In economics, this is referred to as the efficient-market hypothesis.

In the stock market, a stock has three directions in which it can move. A stock price can either move up, down or sideways. In science people say 'every action has a reaction. Dow believed the same thing about the stock market. Everything that happens in the economy, or to a business and their market, will influence the movement of stock prices within that market.

Technical analysts look for trends or movements. There are three different types of trends or movements, as defined by the Dow Theory. Number one is the main movement. This is the overall trend in the market, the long-term trend. This trend can be a few months long or even a few years long. This trend could either be downward, or bearish. The trend can also be upward, or bullish.

Within the main movement, there are other smaller movements. A graph that showed the movement of an index over the last six months might show an overall trend moving in the same direction. If we look closer, 'zooming in' on the chart, then we will see that within the bigger primary trend there will be smaller upward and downward movements that last a shorter amount of time. The next category of movements is called the medium swings. These medium swings may last from a few weeks to a few months. They generally move about 30-60% of the main movement. As a swing trader, you will be looking for trends within this time frame.

If you were to zoom in on the chart even closer, you would see that within even the medium swings, there are upward and downward movements that may only run from a few hours to a few weeks. According to Dow Theory, these are called short swings. While the main movement may be heading in one direction, short swings and medium swings may move up and down. These medium and short swings are the types of movements that swing traders and day traders look for because they are shorter term.

Each of these movements can also be broken down into terms explained by the dynamics of market psychology. The breakdown splits each movement into distinct 'phases', each phase representing an action or reaction from traders as economics events unfold within the market. During the first phase, traders who first see the writing on the wall begin to take a position on a stock, usually going against the grain of what the rest of the market is doing. This phase is called the accumulation phase. During the accumulation phase, not much happens to the price of the stock because most investors are still trading with the current, and those traders who anticipate the change make up only a small percentage of them. After some time, the market begins to catch on that a change is either starting to take place or is about to take place. This phase is when the largest amount of movement happens to the price of a stock. People start to catch on to the coming movement, and mass amounts of investors begin to take a position. This phase is called the public participation phase. Ideally, as a trader, we'd like to get our position before this phase so that we can enjoy the benefits of it. After these first two phases, the trend will play out but eventually it the trend will begin to slow. The third phase starts when the first investors begin to sell off their stocks and leave the position in order to make money elsewhere.

The next important tenet of Dow Theory is the one that we have already discussed, on which the other rules are based. That is the belief in the efficient market hypothesis, which means that all relevant information is already reflected in the price of the stock. According to the Dow theory, every new piece of news or information about a company will be quickly interpreted and reflected in the price of a stock. If new information about a company came out during the trading day, then this information will quickly affect the price of that stock.

When Down was creating his first pamphlets to interpret trends in the stock market, indexes worked a little differently.

Companies were far apart and on opposite sides of the country. When people first began using indexes to measure the overall trend in the economy, they primarily made the index from a combination of railroad companies and manufacturing companies. These different types of complementary companies typically moved in the same direction; if factories were making more money and increasing their output, then railroads would be moving a lot of raw materials and finished product across the country. The Dow Jones Industrial Average was created with this idea in mind. The performance of these companies should be moving in the same direction, on average. When these companies start to move in opposite directions of one another, it is a sign that a change will take place in the market soon. This methodology is still in use and it makes up another part of the Dow Theory. The average of the indexes must be moving in the same direction in order to indicate a trend.

In addition to the indexes moving in the same direction, there is another way to reaffirm the existence of a trend. One of the most basic indicators that swing traders use is volume. Volume is the number of trades made during a given period for a certain stock. There are a number of reasons why people might trade a stock, so if the stock price changes but the volume are low then that doesn't necessarily mean a trend exists. But if the price of stock changes, and there is a high volume meaning that a lot of traders are buying and selling that stock as the price changes, then this is a good indication that you are seeing the beginning of a trend.

The last tenet of Dow Theory has to do with the end of a trend. If you are watching a trend and wondering when it will reverse, trying to anticipate that best time to leave your position, then this tenet is important. If you watch a trend, you will see that the trend often doesn't remain consecutive. There might be small reversals within the larger movement itself. If you react to every one of these small reversals, then you might leave your position at the wrong time. These small dips within the overall trend are referred to as noise; they don't always mean much. Eventually, one of those small reversals will stick and the trend will change. It's very difficult to tell the difference, as the market is making small upwards and downwards movements all the time.

Therefore, according to the Dow Theory, we should assume that the trend is continuing until we have very clear indicators that the trend is ending.

While it is impossible to accurately determine whether a movement is a real reversal or not, technical analysts use different sell signals to make an educated guess on whether they should sell or keep holding. These signals can be helpful in determining the reversal of trends, but more importantly, this will tell you what other traders are watching for when they are anticipating a trend reversal. We'll outline some of the more common sell signals that technical analysts use. Again, it's important to note that these signals don't always tell us the correct answer, and we'll have to consider other indicators and market factors before we make a decision on what position we want to take.

Below, we have an example of a very common sell signal at what could be the reversal of a bear market.

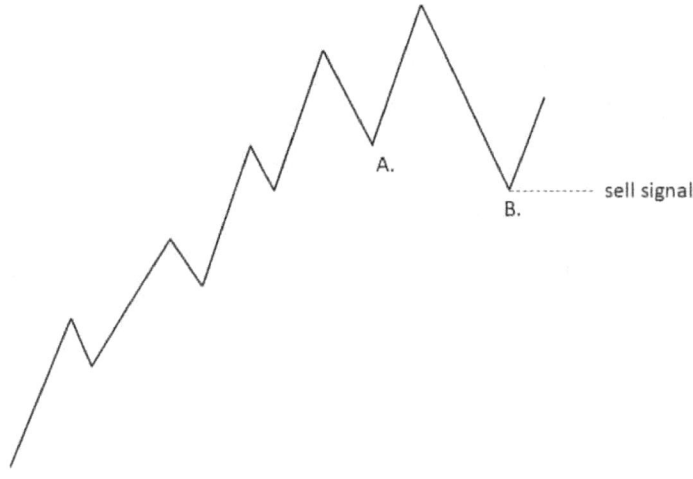

You can see that the market has been bearish for some time, although there is noise in the upward trend. So far you have ridden out the noise and the price of the stock continues to grow, which means if you held on to the stock through these small reversals then you stand to ride with the growth. But how would you know when the reversal is an actual reversal and not just noise? While there is no way to know for sure, there are signs that you can look for. On this chart you see that the stock price has its highest peak after point A, and then drops again to point B. The price of the stock at point B is lower than the last trough and almost as low as the trough before that. For many traders, they would take this as a sell signal because the price of the stock is struggling to rise past its last peak. After point B, the stock price rises again, and you wait. If the stock drops again and reaches point B then this is the place where you will decide to sell.

Whether you decide to use this sell signal, or you decide to continue to wait, understanding these sell signal signals will give you a better picture of what other traders on the market are doing. You may see a high volume of sales of that stock after the price dips below this selling point, which might cause it to dip further. This is an example of why technical analysis and market psychology go hand and hand. The attitude of the market will be reflected in the price of the stock as well as the volume at which it's being traded. Anticipating what other traders are doing will give you a leg up when you are competing on the stock market.

Recall that short sellers make their money on bearish markets by selling high and buying low. This means that they will be watching for reversals when the stock market is on a downward trend because they want to buy at the lowest point, they possibly can in order to make the biggest margin. If they pay back their broker too early, then they will miss out on the potential profits from waiting until the price drops further. Just as traders will use sell signals on a bull market, short sellers will look for signals on a bear market. Those signals will look similar, but the movements will be in the opposite direction. Below is an example of a reversal signal in a bear market; the kind a short sell might look for.

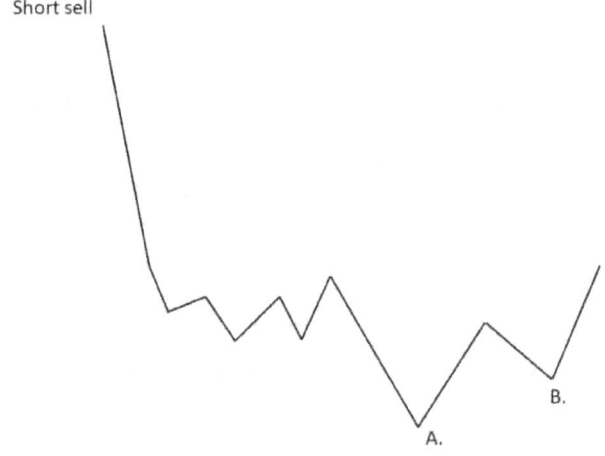

The market drops significantly, and at a very fast rate from where you short sold the stock. You want to maximize your profits though, and the stock might continue to drop so you will wait until you are as close to the floor of the bear market as you can get. The absolute lowest point in the trough as far as we know is at point A. You see that the price moves up again after point A and then does a small reversal and heads back down to point B. For many short-sellers, point B would be a sell signal because the price of the stock failed to drop lower than the lowest trough, which means that the bearish movement might be starting to lose some steam.

Again, there is no way to know with absolute certainty what will happen after point B. It could go down quite a bit further. But, if you are trying to anticipate the attitude of the market then B could be a signal to bullish traders that it's a good time to buy the stock, which means that the price of the stock might continue to rise. Remember to keep track of the volume so that you can try to distinguish noise from reversals.

This type of bearish reversal indicator can also be applied when you are looking to buy a stock, and you want to purchase it at its lowest price. You would wait through a bear market and continue watching to buy right before the trend reverses. So, buy signals and sell signals are very similar; after all the goal is to anticipate the moment when the market turns around and the trajectory changes. In these instances, low relative volumes around the peaks and troughs will give you a clearer picture of whether or not the reversal has any significant power behind it.

The most important thing about technical analysis is the belief that the movements in the stock market aren't completely random. Although there is a degree of randomness, which is why it takes time to learn, there are patterns and traders can learn from those patterns in order to improve their profits. A pattern is when a movement or a series of movement repeat themselves. If you looked at the picture of the stock market over long period of time, you'd see that it moves in cycles. It moves up slowly for a long period of time and then crashes for a while before repeating the process again. Stock traders often use the adage; "what goes up must come down". This is completely true, and the stock market has always followed this pattern. The difficult part of trading, though, knows *when* it will go up or down. Technical analysts are constantly trying to study patterns in order to determine the answer to that question.

Remember that the Dow Theory believes that the stock market is perfectly efficient, which means that the price of a stock will always consider every market factor and it will always reflect the true value of that stock. But there are many traders and investors out there who believe that isn't the case, and they build their entire trading strategies around theories that go against certain tenets of Dow Theory. In fact, there is good evidence that enforces the idea that stocks can be overvalued or undervalued, depending on market factors.

For example, if a certain company is gaining a lot of notoriety, then the price of that stock will likely increase. People will start to see it as more and more valuable, and the price of the stock will reflect that increase in value people have perceived. This can cause a stock to be overvalued, though. This type of overvaluing can be what causes bubbles to form; the value of a stock gets so inflated, and at some point, the bubbles bursts and the value of the stock drops. Afterward, it may take quite a bit of time for the stock to rise back to value before the bubble popped.

On the other hand, it's not unusual for a stock to be undervalued. It might be overlooked by the market even though its dividends and projected growth are solid. A tech company that has made a lot of headlines, promising to bring tourists to Mars in the next ten years will probably pull more investors than a waste management company, even if their fundamentals are the same. As a savvy investor, you shouldn't be afraid to dig a little deeper to try and find stocks like this that are overlooked by other investors. That's why it's important to have a solid understand of fundamental analysis before you start swing trading. It will help you make a more informed decision on what types of stocks you want to choose.

Dow Theory may not apply to all situations, but it's important to understand the concepts if you are trading with a certain psychological strategy in mind. In many cases, you are more focused on what other traders are doing and how the market is moving in patterns, rather than with the actual fundamentals of a company. This can be just as important as fundamentals if you're a swing trader or a day trader through. Oftentimes the upward and downward movements you are hoping for are caused by the market's reaction as well as psychological

The challenge of technical analysis is choosing which indicators work the best for you as a trader. Most technical analysis is a mixture of market psychology and statistics, so not all strategies will work all the time. Traders may rely solely on technical analysis and find success with that approach. Other traders may find that fundamental analysis is the most important tool they have because of the strategies they use. The type of strategies you use and the indicators that you pick will depend on your approach to swing trading. The type of companies and the sector you choose will also play a role because different indicators will be important in different industries.

While only using technical analysis might cause you to overlook the fundamentals of certain companies, fundamental analysis may not always give you a complete picture either. If you only use fundamental analysis, then you would miss an opportunity to study the market psychology and to interpret patterns in the movement of stock prices. If you want to be a dynamic swing trader, then you should have some understanding of both types of analysis. One type of analysis won't give you every relevant indicator. Skilled swing traders will review the fundamentals of a company to make their own evaluation of its health, and then they will take what they know and examine the movement of that stock up until now.

When you choose a stock, you will have to decide which type of strategy will work best with that given stock. Maybe you have a strategy in mind, so you will choose your stock by looking to see if the characteristics of the stock will fit with your strategy. In technical analysis, you will be looking for stocks with certain degrees of volatility so that you can study the historical trends of that stock. Oftentimes day traders will look for stocks based on their movements and the current environment in the stock market rather than on the characteristics of the company. They want to capitalize on the small reversals and adjustments rather than a company that has fundamentals.

If you're using fundamental analysis, then the fundamentals will depend on the length of time that you are willing to hold on to that stock, or whether you want to short sell it or hold it for a long bullish trend. If you want to get on board with a stock that has been hyped up, and you think eventually the stock will have a bubble effect, then you'll be interested in different fundamentals than if you wanted to buy a stock and hold on to it long-term.

If you aren't fixed on a strategy, then choose a company that interests you that you don't mind researching. Read about how current events are impacting the share price of that company, and how the company is performing in the current economy. Decide the strategy you would like to use based on your research and continue to monitor the company's health and progress. If you wanted to buy a business, then think about the economy that the business is trying to survive in. What types of external factors will help or put pressure on that company?

So how can you use technical analysis? The first thing that might want to know is how these types of graphs can be accessed, and how you can keep track of these movements and their volume in real-time. There are several good financial websites that will update you on the stock market in real-time. Most of these websites use the same type of chart. Financial websites tend to be a little bit more detailed than typical line graphs like the ones shown above. Although the financial sites will use a graph that is very similar, there are added elements which show more details about the movements of the stock prices.

The most common type of chart employed by swing traders and day traders is called a candlestick chart. Candlestick charts get their name from their appearance, which looks like candles with wicks coming out at either end. The length of the wicks and the length of the candlestick are certain indicators about the movement of that stocks price. Each candlestick represents a set amount of time, depending on how close you are looking. You can look at candlestick charts that represent a day, a week, or longer. You can look at charts where each candlestick represents the movement of the price of that stock on a given day. The characteristics of these charts will be identical whether you are trading stock indexes, forex, or commodities.

The image below is an example of a candlestick chart. In this chart, black candlesticks represent a decrease while white candlesticks represent an increase. Other charts may come in red and green, with green meaning an increase and red meaning a decrease. As you can see, the basic shape of the candlestick chart is like the shape of the line graphs we viewed earlier. The candlestick chart follows the flow of a line graph but it's broken down into segments which reveal more information about the price movement.

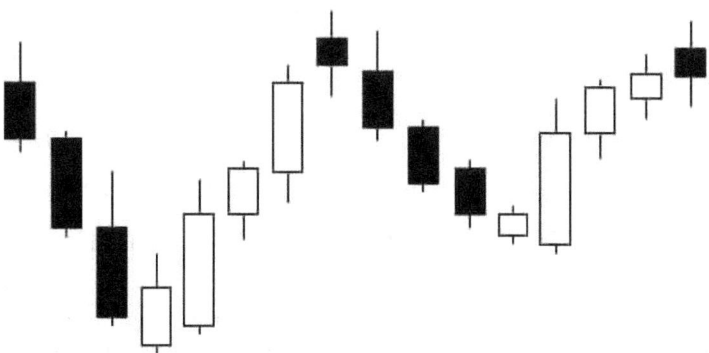

A candlestick chart is a dynamic tool because in one place we can tell a few things about a stock. If we want to break our chart into a day-by-day pieces, then the candlestick can tell us the price of the stock when the market opened, the highest price that the stock reached during that trading day, the lowest price of the stock at the trading day, and the price of the stock when the day closed. The bottom wick is used to show the lowest price of the day and the tops wick stretches up to the highest price of that stock during the same period. The body of the candle follows the wick depending on where it closed throughout the day. If the top of the candle has no wick, then the price of the stock closed at its highest price for the day. If the bottom of the candle has no wick, then it closed at its lowest point for the day.

So, from one chart you can see not only the price of a stock but how it moved throughout the day and through the days preceding. Being able to read a candlestick chart will help you have a clearer picture of the trend that this stock is moving on, and how the market perceives the stock.

When you are trading on the stock market, then you will either take the position of a buyer or a seller. If you haven't decided on what position you'd like to choose, then you exist somewhere in the middle. The stock market works because at any given time there should be buyers and sellers available who are constantly impacting the supply and demand of a stock. The candlestick chart illustrates the movement caused by these two opposing forces; the buyers and sellers. Throughout the day, if there were more buyers than sellers, then the body of the candle will be high and have a short top wick. If there were people trying to offload the stock, and the supply of the stock increased while willing buyers decreased then the candle will have a long body and a short bottom wick.

Remember that technical analysis is all about identifying trends and patterns. In Dow Theory, we talked about how traders look for certain buy and sell signals based on the volume and trajectory of a stock. A candlestick chart will be your best friend in providing you with the information needed to identify the buy and sell points. Remember to keep an eye on the volume of a stock, because trends need to be confirmed by volume even when you are looking at a candlestick chart.

Just as there are technical trends to be identified on a line graph, there are certain patterns that may appear in candlestick charts. The appearance of certain candlesticks in sequence with one another or the frequency of certain types of candlesticks may be indicative of certain movements or trends. The longer a candle is, the more movement there has been in the stocks price.

If the candlestick is long as has a shorter wick on top then the trend for the day was bullish, the meaning it was moving up. If the candlestick is long but the wick on the bottom is short, then the stock price has a bearish trend. Use the volume of the stock to decide whether these movements are noise or if there is a good indication of a trend.

Again, technical patterns on the stock market are not reliable all the time. It's important to emphasize that if this were true, then it would be too easy to predict where the market would go next. If the patterns were always consistent and readable, then trading would be easy money because you could always predict the outcome of a trend. On the other hand, there are some very common candlestick patterns that appear quite frequently. They may not always result in the exact same outcome. Just like all the other indicators we have talked about, these patterns are another indicator that you would use to reinforce your confidence in a position. No indicator is proof by itself, but if the technical indicators and the fundamental indicators match one another then your position will at least be educated and informed.

Candlestick patterns can infer one of two outcomes; they may be a sign that the current trend will continue, or they may be a sign that the trend is about to change or reverse. The type of trend the candlestick predicts depends on the order and shape in which the candlesticks appear.

The following candlestick is a type of reversal that occurs when the market goes from bearish to bullish. In this pattern, there are three black downward-moving candlesticks. The third black candlestick shows that the stock closes very close to its low point. The next day, the stock opens lower than it closed the day before, but it overcomes the last downward candlestick. If you see this pattern during a bearish market, then it is usually a very good sign that the trend is reversing. In most cases this trend will be an accurate prediction of a reversal. This pattern is known as the **three-line strike**.

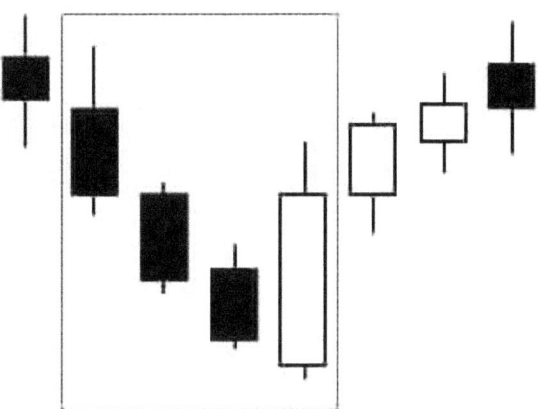

The candlestick pattern in the following picture will usually occur after a peak high. Notice the significant gap between the first two black bars. This means that the stock opened at a price which was significantly lower than the price from the day before. You can see that in this pattern there is an abrupt drop in value that happened after the trading day closed. This type of gap could form outside of trading hours as the result of some piece of news about a company that impacts its stock negatively. Maybe the company released a financial report that wasn't very promising, or the evening news reported a recall on one of their products. This pattern is a very good sign that the price of the stock will continue downward. This pattern is known as two black gapping.

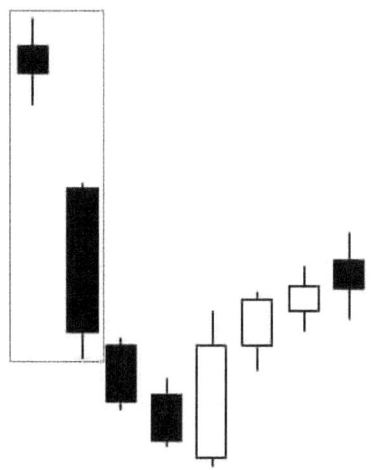

The next candlestick pattern also occurs at the end of a peak, as a bearish reversal pattern. This pattern is denoted by three black candlesticks dropping after a peak. This many consecutive days of significant price drops is a sign that this bearish trend will only continue. Traders will see this and lose confidence in the stock, exiting their positions and further exacerbating and continuing the drop. Most of the time, if you see this candlestick pattern then you can predict with confidence that this trend is going to stick and the stock will remain bearish for some time. This candlestick trend is called three black crows.

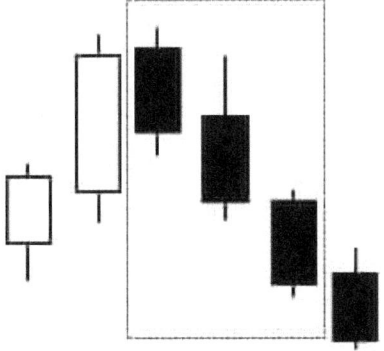

The three black crows are a bearish reversal pattern, there is an opposite reversal pattern which signifies the end of a bearish trend. The following picture shows the end of a bearish pattern followed by three consecutive days of prices trending upwards. Both of these reversal patterns tell us something about the momentum of the stock, and how trader confidence is growing as the pattern continues. In this case, we can have confidence that this bullish trend will continue on a bullish pattern. The downward momentum pattern is called three black crows, while this upward momentum pattern is called three white soldiers.

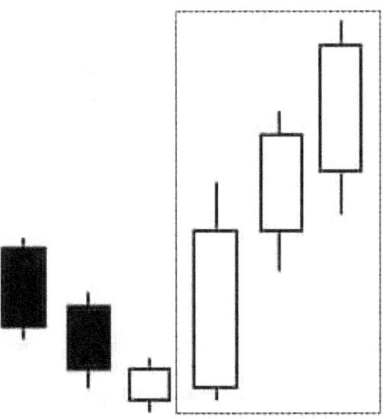

In the next candlestick pattern, the stock price is on an upward trend as denoted by the white candlesticks for the first two days. The following day, traders anticipate the trend will continue so the stock opens at a higher price. In this case, though, the momentum on the upward trend slows down significantly after the price increase and actually goes down by the end of the day. The decrease in trader confidence creates another downward gap on the following day. Usually, this candlestick pattern is an indication that the stock has peaked and will likely not go higher. The failure of the stock to keep its momentum may actually cause it to drop even further in the coming days. This candlestick pattern is called the evening star.

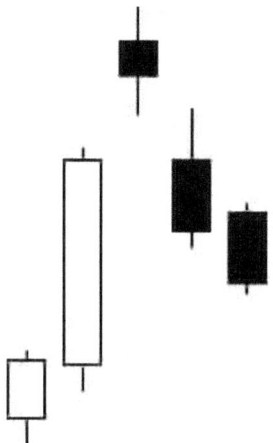

The evening star usually scares investors away because it causes them to anticipate a new downtrend. On the opposite end of the cycle, we have a pattern known as a morning star. The morning star appears at the end of a bearish trend. The morning star is a sign of new hope that inspires investors and gives them confidence after a downward cycle. As you can see in the following picture, the downward trend continues for a while but fails to maintain its momentum at the bottom of the trough. While the morning star alone isn't enough to confirm a reversal, it might inspire the beginning stages of a bullish cycle as traders begin to take positions again as confidence grows.

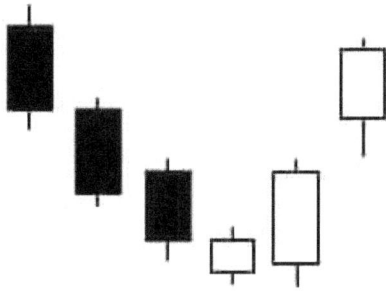

While not all candlestick patterns will be a sure sign on their own, you can combine what you know about these technical patterns with what is happening in the market. While patterns do occur, the market also has enough randomness to keep it from being completely predictable. That doesn't mean there aren't recognizable characteristics of certain trends that are worth taking note of. Being able to recognize these patterns won't be the single answer to trading successfully, but its another tool which you can add to your fundamental analysis and market research to give you a better understanding of the stock market.

Remember that the most important thing you can learn from a candlestick chart is the perception that the market has about a given stock. The movement of a candlestick chart gives us more information than just the change of the stocks price. At any given time, you are not the only trader who is watching stock and trying to anticipate the next move. Millions of other traders are doing the same thing that you're doing; trying to guess what will happen next. If you know how to read a candlestick chart and you can interpret the market psychology correctly, then you'll be in a better position to act on a position.

The tricky thing about the stock market is the way this collective mindset among traders can influence that actual outcome. If a popular analyst puts out a statement that says the price of a stock will go down, and you'd be wise to exit your position on that stock, then you might see a high volume of people selling that stock the next day. The collective psychology of traders does influence the way the prices move. When we talk about trader or investor confidence, we are referring to a collective willingness among traders to start buying a stock. Usually, this collective confidence will spread among other investors, and the belief in a future trend among many traders will make the trend more likely.

This isn't always the case though, and that's a fortunate thing because we make the most money when we see something that the rest of the market doesn't. Short sellers make money when they bet against a company. You make money on a bullish stock when you buy it low, believing that it will soon be worth much more. The fact that traders will often bet in different directions is what makes the stock market so challenging, but what opens the door to profits.

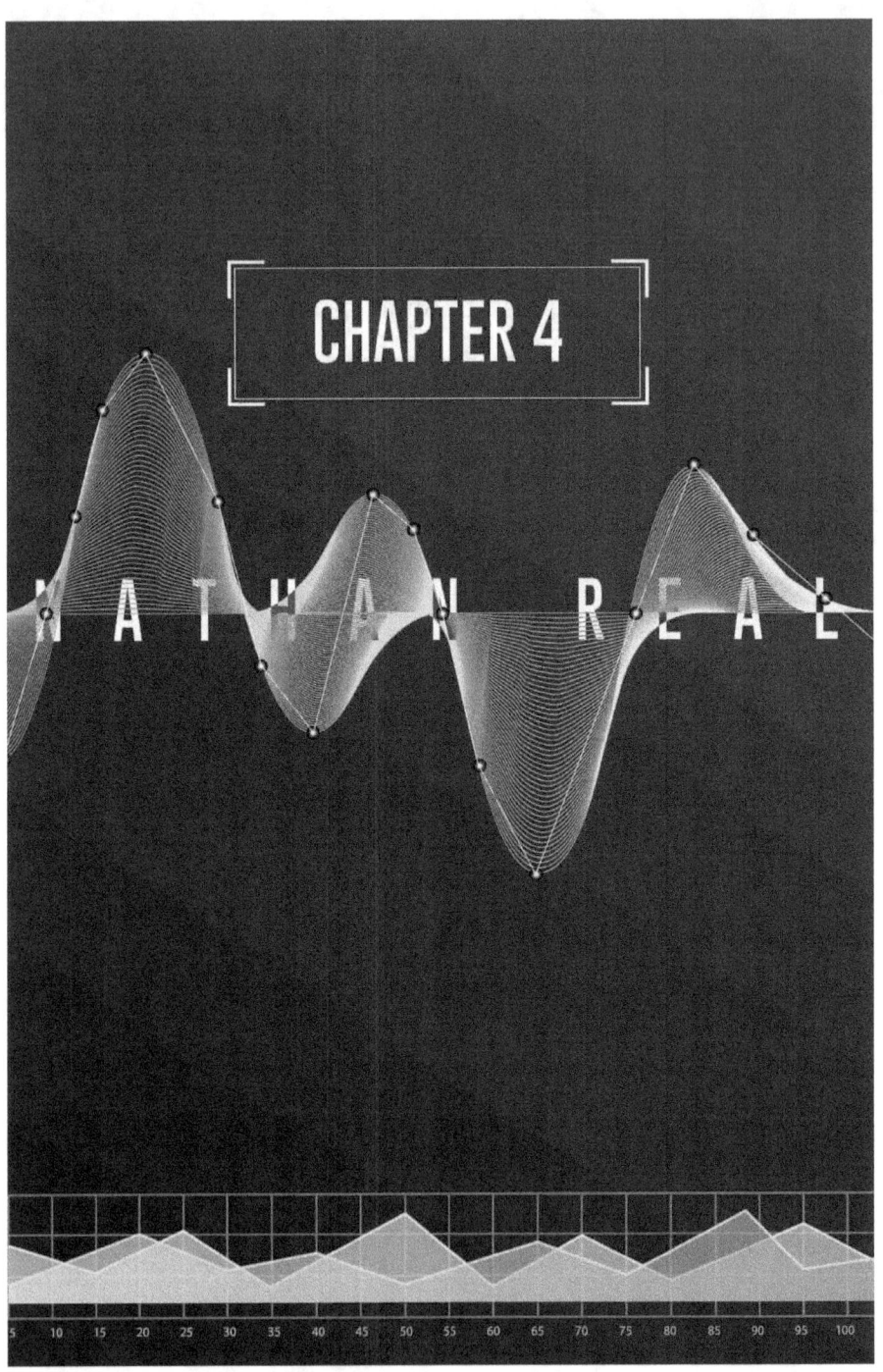

CHAPTER 4

Chapter 4: The Swing Trader

With some understanding of technical analysis and fundamental analysis, you will already be ahead of most beginner traders when you enter your first trade. Beyond the research you can do, there are a handful of other aspects of trading that often get overlooked but that will become obvious over time. These things fall into the category of "stuff you wish someone had told you when you started swing trading". Luckily, this book is here to help.

Swing trading is like a test that requires constant studying a revision. You should treat it like an important test or an important paper that requires good research. If you research effectively, then you will profit. If you get lazy with your research, then you might miss obvious signs that would have led you to make a different decision in the first place.

On the flip side of that, don't get slowed down by trying to find a position that ticks all boxes of a perfect bet. You should be detailed with your research, but ultimately there are some trades where you will need to trust your gut above all else. This is a skill that is developed over time, and so you will get better at it. But you won't be able to analyze every technical and fundamental element on every trader.

This is where things like organization and good record keeping come in to play. As you enter more and more positions, you will notice certain indicators that will match your mindset and your strategy better than others. Sure, there are no indicators that are 100% foolproof, so don't try to look for those either. But your mindset and the type of trading you engage in will make some indicators more important than others. As you learn to trade more efficiently, you will know which indicators to look for right away based on the characteristics of a certain company. Don't forget about all the other indicators, but in some instances, there are certain indicators which she is highlighted about the others. If things don't line up with your strategy, don't force yourself to take a position just for the sake of trading. Start out with fewer, smaller trades and slowly expand your trading as you learn and practice. Stay organized and focused and eventually it will come together.

If you choose to participate in swing trading over other types of trading, then you are probably most interested in the time frame that swings trading presents. You are more flexible than both a day trader and a long-term position investor. If things are going well, you don't have to remove yourself from a position the way a day trader will. If things are going poorly then you don't have to ride out the roller-coaster cycles the way a position investor has to. Your advantage over the long-term investor is to seek opportunities that look good at that moment, rather than keeping your capital tied up in long term prospects.

In addition to these advantages you are also susceptible to risks that are unique to a swing trader. Because you hold your position longer than a day trader, the effects of a bad trade will be drawn out and may result in higher losses. The day trader can respond to any movements or price changes because all their positions last less time than a day. A swing trader is more likely to hold a position overnight. Even though the stock market closes, the price of stocks can change after hours. If this happens then you are stuck holding your position whether that position is a good one or not.

Remember that the stock market represents shares in companies that operate and exist outside of the stock market. Business news and company developments don't turn off for the day just because the stock market closes. A company could put out a press release that significantly affects the price of stock even after the market has already closed, leaving investors nervously sitting on their hands until the market opens again. Examples of events that could shape stock price after hours include secondary offerings and financial releases. You will have to be aware of the impact these could have on your position.

When a company issues stock, it usually doesn't release all the available shares at once. The company will hold on to a certain number of shares in the case it needs to generate capital in the future. By selling more shares later, the company will generate extra cash. This is common if a public traded company is trying to expand a product line or invest in a new development. By introducing a secondary offering at the right time, the company can get cash on hand fast.

If you're a shareholder though, the secondary offering may damage your portfolio. We've established that the price of a stock is the result of interactions between supply and demand. When a company releases a secondary offering, then the supply of the stocks will increase. An increase in the supply of something typically results in a decrease in price to find the equilibrium price point between supply and demand.

The impact of a secondary offering will depend on the position you've taken as well as the number of shares released. Sometimes the secondary offering won't be large enough to impact the price of the stock in any significant way. A small increase in the percentage of shares available may not make a big difference. But if the secondary offering is quite large then it can significantly devalue your position.

The problem is, you can't anticipate a secondary offering because companies won't announce it ahead of time. Sometimes you think you have found a good position and the company will announce a secondary offering out of nowhere. But, its an added element to be aware of if you keep a good eye on the fundamentals of your company. If a company is struggling to bring in revenue, but they are talking about expanding certain lines of their business then this company is more likely to make a secondary offering. Again, there is no way to know for sure but there are warning signs that lay in the fundamentals of a company, and now you know to keep your eyes peeled.

The next thing to watch for is financial releases or statements about the company's earnings. The good thing about these is that the company will announce them ahead of time, so you can plan around them. They always happen after the market is always closed but they still impact the way your position opens the following day. If the company announces their revenue and they are showing signs of growth, then you'll be happy you were holding a position in that stock. If the company announces stagnant growth or a decline in growth, then the results of that announcement will be reflected in the price of the stock on the following day. You can either see this as an opportunity or avoid holding positions during financial announcements, depending on your confidence in the company. Either way it's something that's worth knowing about if you plan on becoming a swing trader.

You should pay close attention to what analysts say about a stock, before and after you buy it. What they predict may come true but more importantly, what they predict may encourage certain movements among investors. They may also make predications after the market closes that will affect the value of your positions on the following day. This could either be a benefit to you or it could hurt your portfolio; keep yourself updated on what the analysts are saying so you don't wake up to any surprises when the market opens.

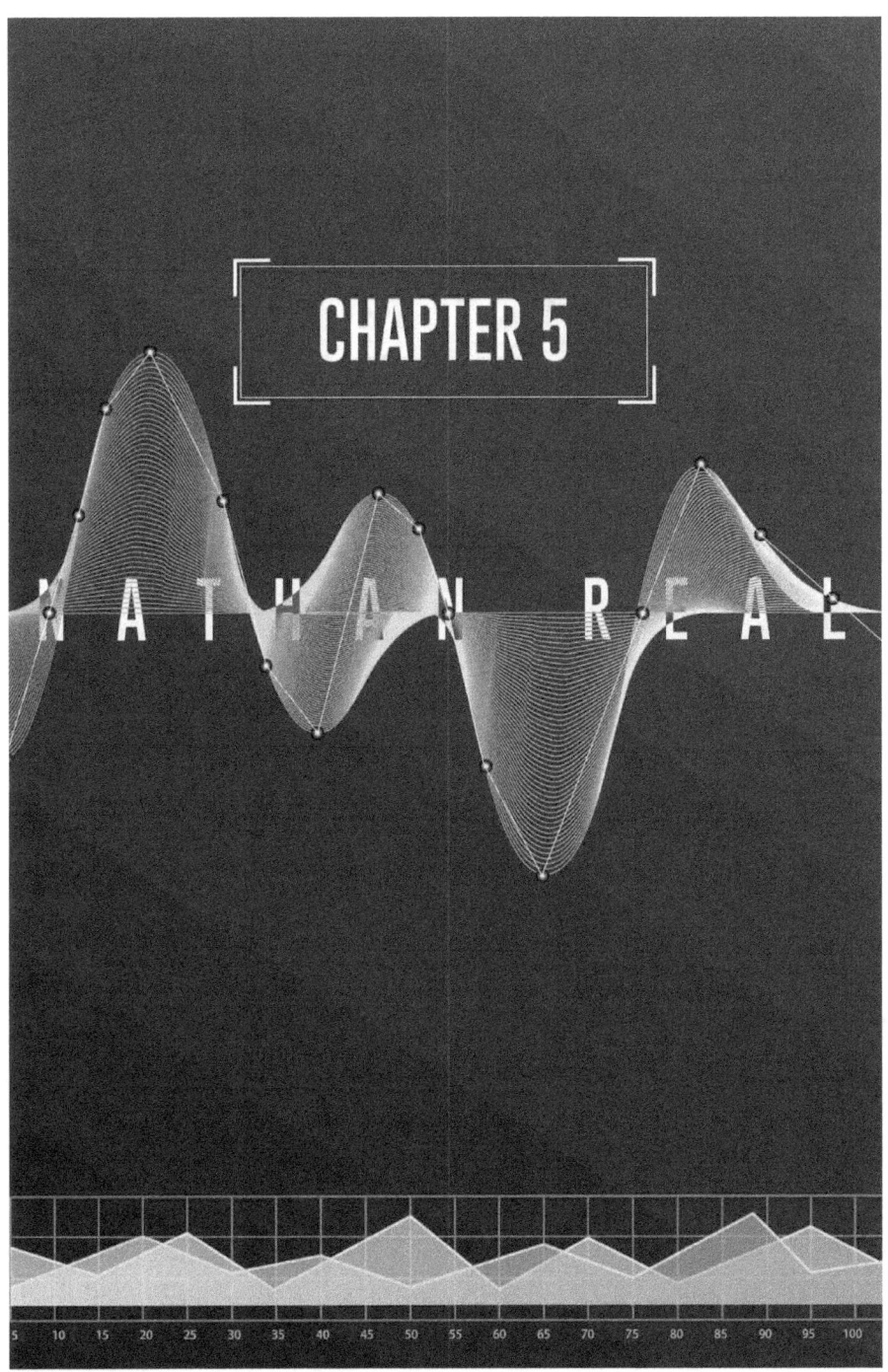

CHAPTER 5

NATHAN REAL

Chapter 5: Strategies for Swing Traders

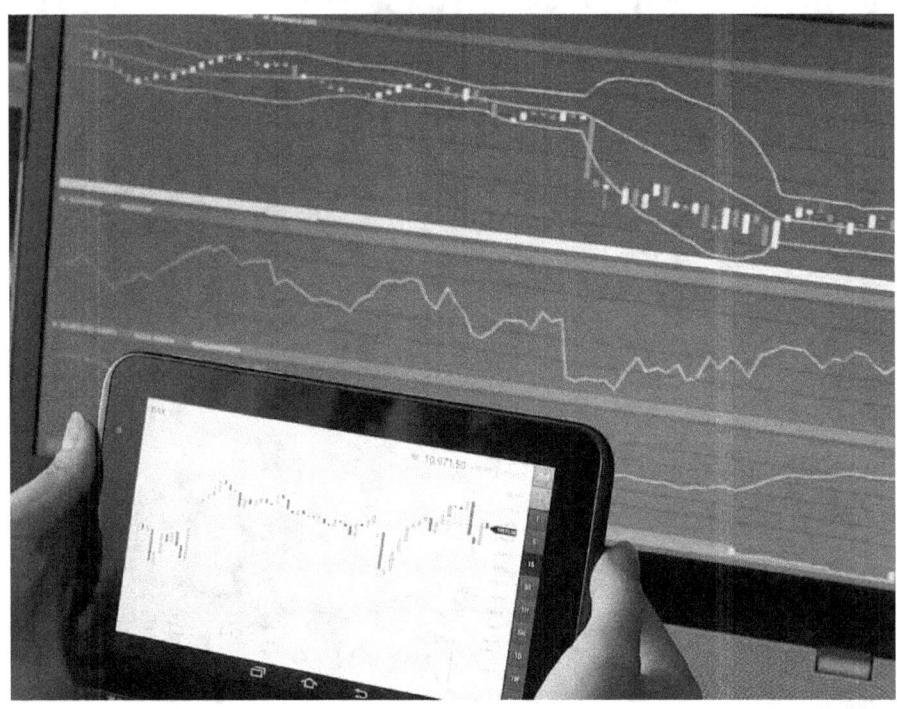

You've probably been reading this book and wondering at what point we will start to talk about swing trading strategies. After all, you are probably most interested in the actual strategies that you can apply to make money swing trading. You can see though, that there is a lot to learn before you can start to understand the strategies that people use to swing trade. The market has many factors at play, and you need to understand the tools used to assess companies and their technical movements. You won't be able to use the same strategy in every situation, so knowing how to read the market is the first step before learning strategy.

The indicators that you are looking for will depend on the type of strategy you are using, so pay close attention to the fundamental characteristics of companies and you'll start to recognize similarities amongst different opportunities.

The first step is to make a habit of mining for opportunities. There are a lot of fascinating economic and business journals available on the internet that you can peruse for information about current events and finance news. You never know how you will identify your next opportunity. An article about energy companies in Texas may inspire you to research energy contracts in the American Southwest, and which companies to watch for. An article in a tech news magazine might send you on a hunt for publicly traded companies developing a certain type of computer hardware. If it intrigues you, then let yourself be drawn in for further research. The important thing is to spend a little time each day reading and identifying possible opportunities. Once you've noticed an opportunity, dig a little deeper and review the company's involved and check out their fundamentals. How have these companies been performing? Is it worth taking a position?

You can do this research by looking at the market sector by sector. Find indexes that represent different sectors you are interested in and check up with them every day. It's good to have a relatively broad field of interests from which you can identify options. One sector might be ripe with opportunities while another sector lags on the same day. Being able to switch gears and focus on the place where opportunities are happening will make you a more effective and well-rounded trader.

The type of strategy you use will also affect what characteristics you'll be looking for. If you are willing to take on a little more risk and you want to try swing trading, then you will be looking for stocks that show signs of a moving downwards. With the uptick rule, you will have to find stocks that are moving up now, but you have reason to believe that they will continue to drop in the future.

If you want to buy a stock and hang on to it and make a profit, then you'll be looking for stocks or sectors that are healthy and have continued and consistent growth. The earlier you enter a position, the better. Look out for signs of reversals as both a short seller and a bull trader. The sooner you enter a position after a true reversal, the more you can earn.

Remember the tenet of Dow Theory that states that the average of all the stocks in the index should confirm each other. You may just take a position on one or two stocks, but its good to have a picture of the entire sector. This will tell you whether you will be swimming upstream or downstream. It's OK to swim upstream as long as you feel like you have a compelling reason.

When you have identified a stock that balances risk and reward ratio, decide what price you'd like to buy-in. This will require some research into the fundamentals of a company so you can evaluate whether you are overpaying or underpaying.

One strategy that you can employ as a swing trader is known as gap trading. In the last chapter, we discussed gaps that can open between trading days. A gap is when there is a significant difference between the closing price of a stock today, and the opening price of that stock tomorrow. As a swing trader, you can try and take advantage of these gaps by anticipating that gap and choosing a favorable position. There are instances when the gap could go against you; like with a secondary offering or a bad financial report. But there are just as many instances when you can try to predict a gap.

Swing traders have an advantage over day traders because they can use this gap. Day traders are also less susceptible to the risk that the gap creates. Depending on your outlook and your strategy, you may see the gap as either a good thing or a bad thing. Unfortunately, with gap trading, you don't have much control if the stock price moves against your position. You just must wait for the market to open the next day in order to react.

Gaps could open in several ways. A company could release a statement of earnings, and as a result, the price of the stock could drop or go up significantly in a short amount of time. Unfortunately, it's hard to anticipate a company's earnings report in order to make an educated guess on a good position. Most investors consider it to be too risky to play the gap on an earnings report because it's too easy for there to be a surprise when the company releases its statement.

Another way to take advantage of a gap is by researching companies that are developing new technologies. This type of stock can be very volatile, with attitudes changing swiftly about the predicted success or failure of the product. The volatility could be an opportunity for the swing trader if they timed it right. Just be aware of the way the market can respond to an announcement about new technology. The stock price may shoot up to unprecedented levels as a result but often, things will settle down shortly after. Knowing how to time a position during a product announcement will be a major factor in whether you stand to make any money.

Remember; not all products succeed either. Sometimes a new product can hurt the company, in the long run, more than it helps them in the short run. Imagine an automotive company that announces the release of a new model. For a while, the model could increase anticipated earnings and investors might flock to the company. But the first model of the car might have more issues than expected, and the safety rating may be lower than normal. Remember that Dow Theory says that every action results in a reaction on the market. A product that performs poorly can do just as much harm as a product that performs well. Keep track of the progress of the companies in your portfolio, and make sure you time your positions well.

Another way a swing trader can ride a trend is to seek industries that are experiencing booms. Look for industries that are 'trendy'. Right now, the marijuana industry is experiencing a major boom and investors who recognized the possibilities of this trend early are enjoying a growing portfolio. With the legalization of Marijuana in Canada and many states in the US, there are new companies popping up all over as demand for the product is growing. Eventually, there could be a bubble once the expansion adjusts. But trends like these present opportunities for swing traders. Whether or not you decide to invest in the marijuana industry, its an example of a rideable trend. Who knows how it could play out?

These opportunities that exist in trends don't come around too often, and a swing trader must be patient in order to identify them. Usually, though, all one needs to do to find out about these trends is read the newspaper. Trends come and go and the window for making a real profit is limited. But if you're patient then there will always be another trend around the corner. The trick is to keep your ears to the wind so that you know when an opportunity has arrived.

Just like any swing trading strategy, a lot of it comes down to timing. A good example of a famous trend is the dotcom bubble in the 90s and early 2000s. A lot of people made big off the rise in internet technologies and computer companies. Eventually, though, the trend took a major dip and there were just as many losers from the dot-com trend as there were winners. Just remember that the stock market works in cycles and patterns, and these patterns often repeat themselves. Monitor your positions and stay up to date on news cycles.

When it comes to deciding on a position, timing is important. This means not only timing your exit but also timing your entry. It's better to be patient and wait for a good opportunity to buy when the stock price is low than to try and rush in out of impatience.

Before you open a position decide how much you are willing to pay. This is important because when you have a target price you can calculate exactly what you are risking before you even take on a position. Again, it's better to figure this out before you even take the position. Once you've determined an entry point then you must be patient. Wait for the price of the stock to match your ideal price. If it doesn't, then move on. Never forget that being a good trader requires discipline, which includes knowing when you should take an opportunity and when you should look at other options.

There are ways to track the price or set entry points without the need to constantly monitor the market. For example, a lot of brokerages offer alert services where you can receive notifications when the price of a stock has reached a predetermined target. You decide on an entry point and go about your day, then you receive a notification from your broker. You can even give them a limit order, which tells your broker to buy the stock for you once it hits that target. These notifications are also available for sale targets, so your broker can let you know when the stock has reached that target. They can even sell it automatically for you.

You've read about setting an exit point by now, and how sometimes you'd like to leave some flexibility in case the stock price continues to move in your favor. One way to do this is by not exiting your position all at once. Let's say you a buy a stock and the price of that stock has risen beyond your exit point and it is still moving. You want to preserve some of your earnings, but you are also curious about how high the stock might go. You

take to exit your position with only a portion of your money
while leaving the rest in. You slowly withdraw your position in
increments, but you maintain some percentage of your position
until you are completely ready to withdraw. This technique is
called scaling out.

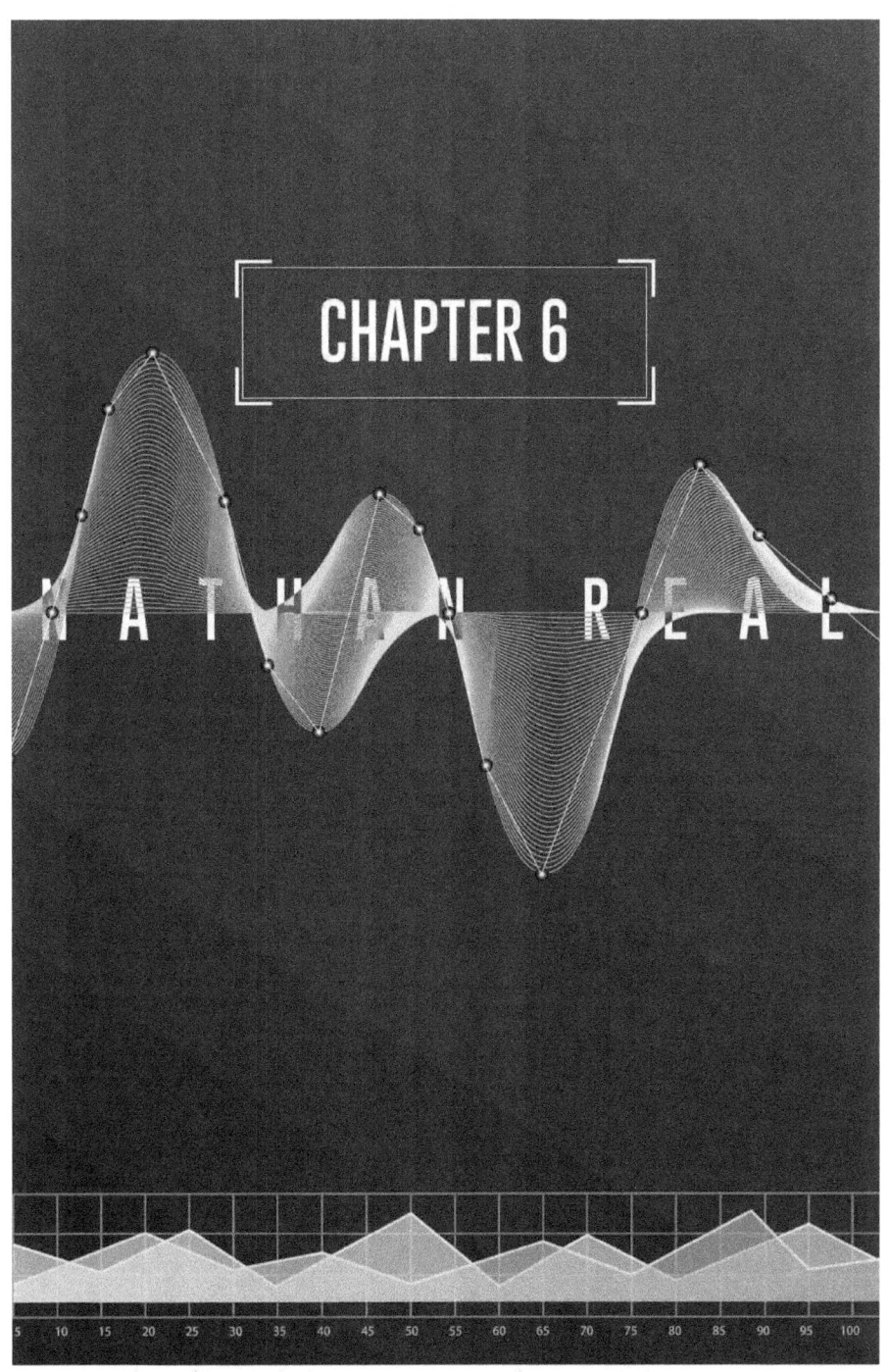

CHAPTER 6

NATHAN REAL

Chapter 6: Protecting Your Capital

There is no way around it; if you want to get involved in swing trading then you will have to put up some of your hard-earned money, risking it in the hopes that you make a profit. In order to play on the stock market, you have got to be willing to take some risks. If you are totally risk-averse, then swing trading isn't for you. It's healthy to be afraid of risk. You never want to lose your money, even if you're willing to put up with some risk. The trick to being a successful trader knows how to evaluate risk levels. When is the risk too high, and when should you cut your losses?

Before you even open an account, you should take time to consider how much risk you are willing to take. You should never put money in the stock market that you can't afford to lose. If you have a bad trade and your portfolio takes a hit, there are still bills to be paid and mouths to feed. Assess how much money you are willing to put into your account when you are first starting.

There are dozens of strategies and tools to help you make money on the stock market, and we've already discussed many of them in this book. There are just as many strategies which are crucial to minimizing risk and minimizing losses. Before you even begin a trade, you should establish an exit point so that when a trade results in a loss, you keep the loss to a minimum. After all, the money you lose is less money you will have to invest with later.

One of the most challenging aspects of investing in the psychology of defeat. You did your research, chose a stock, and decided on a position. After using some of your cash to pay for that position you began to see that the stock market moved against you. You were confident about your bet, but now as the market moves you are losing money. It could turn around, maybe you should wait it out. But if you wait, then you might just lose even more money. If you continue to wait your losses have only really occurred 'on paper'. But once you exit a position on a loss, you are making that loss real. When you finally decide to exit, you exit the position with less money than you started. If you keep waiting though, the market could continue to move against you and your stubbornness will only make it worse.

It's one of the most difficult parts of being a trader, acknowledging that you were wrong and backing out and moving on. In order to combat this, you must be disciplined and create an exit strategy for yourself. This means setting a stop-loss point where you commit to exiting before the trade even begins. If you buy a stock at x amount, deciding that if the stock price drops so many percentage points below x then you will cut your losses and leave the position.

If you start swing trading after reading this book and you stick with it, then there is no doubt that will incur a loss at some point. It's a part of swing trading that you should accept before you begin. If you accept this now, then you are more likely to take a step back and recognize when you decided on a bad position. But in the heat of the moment, the frustration of a loss might take over and you may find yourself struggling with what to do.

Most traders will set a stop loss point that is 6-8% below the price they bought the stock for. Choosing a stop loss point between 6-8% is ideal because it's not a huge amount to lose. If you lose 6-8% of your invested capital in a bad position, it's not hard to make that amount back on a good trade. If you let the loss become much more than that, you will have a hard time gaining that money back. You'll have to have an even more profitable trade in the future in order to just get back to where you started. I often choose 6-8% as a stop loss point because I am confident that I can make that amount back with just a few successful trades. The key is to keep your losses low enough so that you can keep trading and make that money back.

It can be difficult to force yourself to stick with the stop-loss plan. Being a good trader requires a cool, disciplined head especially in times of a loss. If you have these personality traits then you are more likely to keep your head down when things aren't going well and stick with your original plan, which means you'll be in a better position to trade again later and hopefully have profitable trades in the future. Remember that this is what makes swing trading advantageous for a beginning trader. While things may unfold quickly for a day trader, things move slower when you are swing trading.

The other question to ask before you enter a position is how much you can make, and how much can I lose. If I see an opportunity to make $100 that requires me to take a position that costs $200, then this position isn't worth it because I'm risking twice as much money as I can make. Most trades will consider the risks compared to potential rewards when picking up a new position. For any type of trader, you should only take positions where the inverse is true. If you have the potential to make twice as much as you stand to lose, then this is a better bet and the risk is more worth it.

Evaluating the risk of any given trade is the first thing any trader should do before taking a position. How volatile is the price of the stock you are taking a position on? Volatility is the frequency at which the stock moves up and down, and it can be a good indication of the risk involved with investing in that stock. If a stock has a lot of upward and downward movement then there is the potential that this stock may result in profits, but it also comes with a higher degree of risk. The more volatile a stock is, the higher the risk associated with trading that stock.

If you choose a position, and things are working in your favor, then you will need to consider how long to ride the trend in order to maximize the profit you make on that position. If you buy a stock and the price keeps rising, how long should you hold onto it before you sell? You might choose a target for your profit but get cold feet and back out before the stock price hits that level, fearing that if you wait too long then you will miss out on what you've already gained. After all, when the stock price is moving in a favorable direction for your position, you have only made money 'on paper' until you exit the position.

So, you should pick a target to exit, even on a positive trade. You should stick with your plans and choose your stop-loss and exit points carefully. But in the case of an exit point on a profitable trade, there is, of course, more flexibility. If you are willing to keep monitoring the stock and continuously reevaluate then you can be more flexible with your exit target. If you have a good reason to believe that the stock will continue to go up beyond the exit point you've chosen, then you should plan to ride it. Just be ready to exit the position quickly, and make sure you're able to stay close to a chart.

Remember that in these moments a lot of the decision comes down to our fundamental and technical indicators. This means that you must stay up to date with the goings-on of a company whose stock you've chosen a position on, and you should be able to read a candlestick chart to look for signs that the market perception of that stock is about to change. Anticipating the moves of other traders will help you decide when you think a trend is about to reverse, and when it's a good time to exit.

The last major part of managing risk involves knowing how much you should stake in a certain position. We've already talked about managing the risk/reward ratio on a potential position. But what percentage of your total capital should you stake on any one position? It's generally a bad idea to risk your entire capital by putting all your money in one position. This is a key part of diversification. Not putting all your eggs in one basket is the golden rule of trading and the most important part of managing risk.

It's true of swing trading that some of your trades will make you a profit, and some trades will end in a loss. So, it makes sense that diversification is the best way to making a profit overall on the aggregate of all your positions.

Most investors choose to use what is known as the one percent rule. You should never put more than 1% of your total account on any single position. If I had an account with $100,000 then I should never risk more than \$1000 on any one position. Unfortunately, following this rule can be very difficult if your investment capital is much smaller. If you only have \$5,000 in your account, then you can only put \$50 on any one trade. So obviously this rule will be easier for traders with larger accounts.

Sometimes a trader may feel especially confident about a potential opportunity that they've identified. They might decide that in a certain case, it's worth it to break their own rules. It can be easy for investors to get caught in this trap, thinking that they've found a path to easy money and as a result they put more than they should have into one position. But the market often goes against what we expect. There is always the chance that something that appeared to be a sure bet turns out to be a lemon. The overconfidence that easy money could be had results in heavy losses.

Always remember that risk is a factor in every position. A wise investor will try to mitigate the damage from risk, rather than avoid it altogether. But a major distinction between traders who fail and traders who succeed is the fact that successful traders have a better understanding of the risks at play in the market. A seasoned trader will rarely break the rules as a result of overconfidence.

Being a profitable trader is not about hitting it big on investments where you outwit the market and discover some massive untapped opportunity. That idea may get popularized in movies like The Big Short, where traders made a fortune off one good position. This type of opportunity is actually very rare. Good traders are people who can manage many smaller positions at once and who have a higher number of profitable trades than trades resulting in a loss. A caveat to that is knowing how to minimize the damage when you do incur a loss and doing their homework to study the market and find several good opportunities at once.

Something that helps many successful traders is keeping a detailed record of all the trades you participate in. It not only will help you keep your position straight in your mind, but it will also give you something to refer to. You'll be able to see what worked and what didn't. If you can keep an organized and detailed record of your trades, then you can iron out your strategies with different types of stocks.

For every trade I participate in, I will take note of several things. If I rely on fundamentals to identify opportunities with certain stocks, I will make a record of which stock I was studying and what the fundamentals looked like when I took my position. I'll probably even make a note of technical details and the performance of the stock throughout the time that I held my position; opening and closing prices, as well as the trading volume of the stock that I held.

You may pick stocks for a variety of reasons. The reasons may be purely formulaic; you choose a stock based on certain fundamental indicators or based on the technical characteristics of the stocks price movement. Whatever means you use to choose a stock; you will be making a bet on that stock's future performance. So, for every stock you take a position on, you should record why you chose the position you did in addition to the performance of the stock. Did it match your expectations? If the stock didn't perform in the way that you expected, were there factors that you overlooked that would have affected your decision to take on a certain position? Do you believe there were any external or internal factors which affected your success on this trade? If there were external or internal factors, what were they?

Over time you will begin to get a feel for what indicators matter the most, and which ones fit the best with your strategy. If you keep a record of your trades, then you might notice patterns with certain kinds of stocks or certain fundamentals. The best education for a trader experiences, so you should try to get the most out of your experience by paying close attention to the factors which affect the success of your trades.

Of course, your trade journal should also include a record of which trades were successful and which trades were not, as well as your profits. How much did you pay for a position, and at what price did you exit the position? You'll start to see what your success record is. If you want to be a profitable trader, then you need to have more successful trades than trades that resulted in a loss.

The best day traders will be organized and detailed. Remember, this is real money you are investing in. Like treating stock as if you were buying the whole business, you should approach trading as if it is a serious job. It requires diligence and clear thinking as well as an organized and rational approach to your decision-making process. The better your research is, and the better your records are, the more likely you will be to learn and improve as a trader.

If you maintain an organized and logical manner of trading, then you are less likely to succumb to the stress that is associated with trading. Trading requires you to think on your feet and make intuitive decisions with limited information about the perceived outcomes. If you are organized and diligent then it will be easier to make these decisions with confidence, rather than in a state of stress.

While you must be able to accept the risk, you should go into every trade with the intention of making money on that trade.

You should never enter a trade with a reckless you-only-live-once type strategy. You might make a good profit on one or two trades if you use this method, but most of the time you will lose because you didn't do your research, or you were overconfident in a position.

The stress from potential or real losses and the quick thinking that is required of a trader can make it easy to burn out in this job. People who thrive under pressure are more inclined to succeed and stick with it because they will accept the job for what it is and make decisions without dwelling too much on fear or doubt. There is risk, and some fear of risk is healthy. You should never accept risk blindly or just for the sake of taking a risk. The risk should serve a purpose or have some potential for a positive outcome.

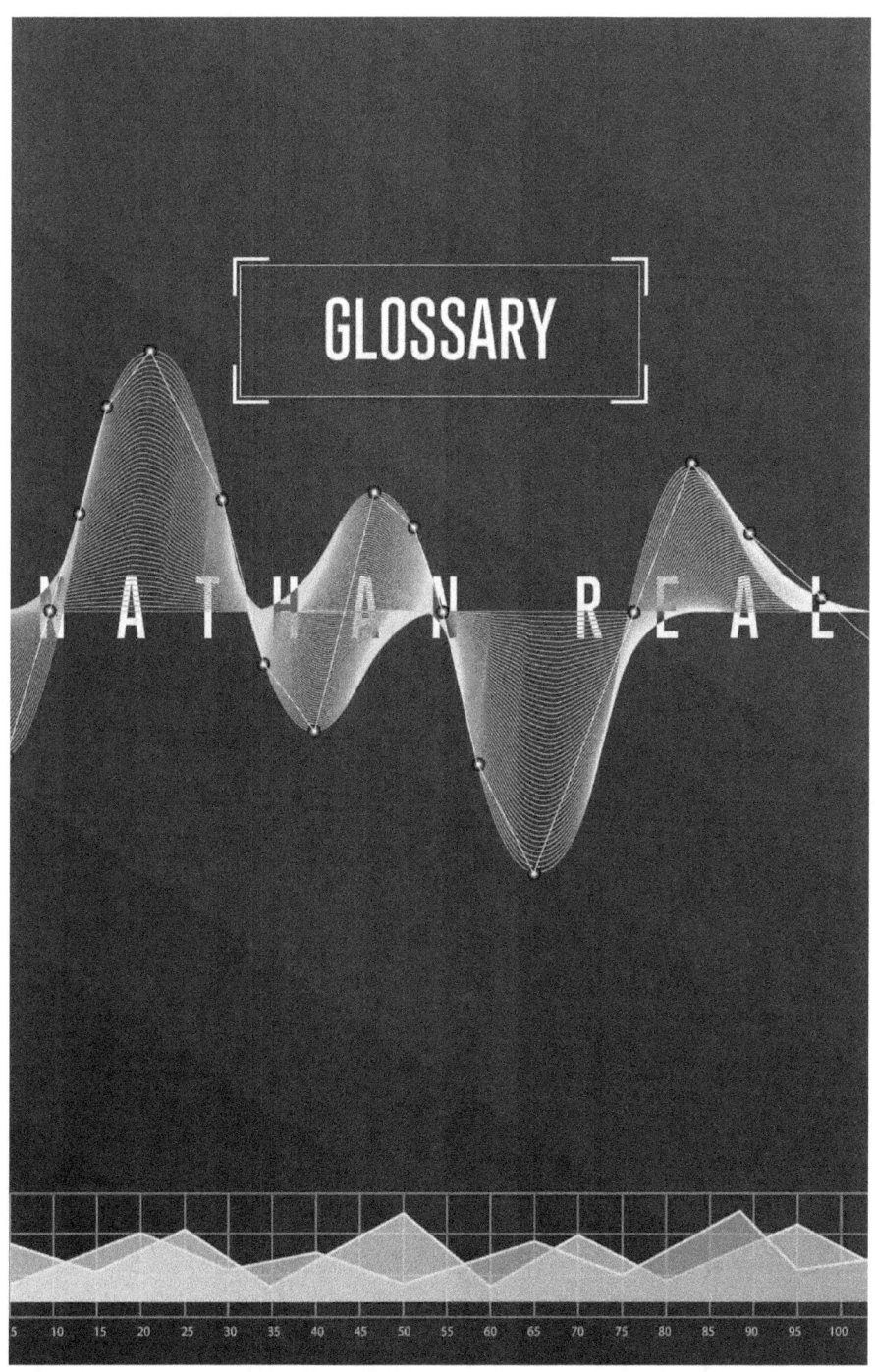

GLOSSARY

NATHAN REAL

Glossary

Anticipation - it is the act of a stock trader predicting about the security market future before either buying or selling of his or her stock.

Asking Price - an initial price at which the security can either be sold for by the investor in the security market
Bearish Stock; a form of stock that is anticipated to decrease in value over a specific time by a stock market trader.

Assignment – this is the process of issuing an option seller or writer with an exercise notice instructing him to sell or buy 100 shares of particular equity at a stipulated amount as the strike value.

At the Money – an 'at the money' option is one that has a cost that is equivalent to the equity's value.

Automatic Exercise – this refers to the process where options that are in the money are exercised automatically, if still in the money during expiration.

Breakeven Point – the point at expiration where an option strategy returns zero profit and zero loss.

A Bearish – market expectation that the value or price of an option will decline over time.

Bear Market – when the overall prices of a market are on the decrease.

Bear Spread – a spread that aims at generating profit from bearish price movements.

Bid Price - it is the highest price of securities such as stocks in the security market a dealer is willingly prepared offer in exchange for the securities.

Bid-Ask Spread – the value obtained from calculating the difference between an option's ask and bid prices.

Black Scholes Pricing Model – model that uses factors such as the value of the underlying security, strike price, time value, and volatility to estimate the price and profits made from options.

Broker – (*definition 1*) a person or organization that processes option contract orders on behalf of traders and investors.

Broker - (*definition 2*) the professional who is responsible for either buying or selling of securities such as stocks for his or her clients.

Brokerage - an individual or a firm responsible for arranging transaction of buying and selling of securities for the sake of getting commission after the exchange is successful.

Bullish – a market state defined by the possibility of the cost rising in future.

Bullish Stock - a type of stock that is predicted to rise in value over a certain period of time by a stock trader in the security market.

Bull Market – state when the overall market prices are increasing.

Bull Spread –trading spread established with the aim of generating profit from bullish stock and market movements.

Buy to Close Order – an order generated when a trader wants to close an existing call position. This is achieved through purchasing contracts that you previously sold to other investors.

Buy to Open Order – this is an order that you place if you want to enter a new position of purchasing contracts.

Call Option - the kind of option that gives a buyer some authority to buy 100 shares for given equity at predefined prices and expiration periods.

Carrying Cost - the cost incurred when using capital to buy options based on the interest received from borrowed capital.

Cash Account - one of brokerage accounts where an investor is required to make full payments of the securities he or she has purchased.

Cash-Settled Option – an option where profits are given to the holder in terms of cash, not in the form of shares.

Close – end a trading position. Also refers to the time of the day when the market stops to operate and the final option prices are determined.

Closing Order – an order that you raise to end a contract that is already in existence.

Combination Order – an order that comprises of more than one basic order.

Contingent Order –an order that allows you to set customized parameters for entering or exiting options contracts.

Contract Range –the highest prices of a single contract minus its lowest prices.

Contract Size – the number of share units covered by individual contracts. In options trading, the default size is 100 shares.

Covered Call - a trading strategy used to make profits from existing contracts when the market is neutral.

Covered Put – a trading strategy that works together with short selling to make profits from existing positions. This strategy protects your investment from short-term price increments.

Currency Option – a form option that has currency as the equity.

Commission – money you give to brokers or brokerage companies for their services.

Credit – the amount of money you get in your account for selling an option.

Day Trader - A person who purchases or sells securities in the security market within a span of a single day.

Debit – the amount of money you give out when purchasing an option.

Derivative – an instrument, which obtains its value from other financial instruments. For example options and futures.

Discount Broker – a broker that only carries out basic order processing for options traders.

Discount Option – an option that sells at a price that is less than the intrinsic value.

Dividend Yield - a form of dividend that is illustrated in form of percentage of the present share price.

Dividends Pay Out Ratio - it is the relative amount of the total revenue that a company pays its shareholders.

Dividends - these are the returns that are paid by a company which an individual owns shares in it.

Early Assignment – when a contract seller fulfills the requirements of the contract before its expiration period.

Early Exercise – the process of closing contracts before they expire.

Earnings Per Share - The portion of the profit made by a firm which is allocated to each share that is out standing in the firm's common stock.

Equity Ratio - A ratio that portrays of how much assets in a firm are being funded by the equity shares.

Exchange Trading Funds - Funds invested for trading in the stock exchange trade.

Exercise – buying or selling an options contract at a specific strike price and time period.

Exercise Price – the price of each share at which it is sold or bought at expiration. This is another name for the strike price.

Expiration Date – The date when a contract stops to exist or expires.

Expiration Month – the month in which expiration takes place.

Expire Worthlessly – a contract that expires worthless is one that returns no profit at the expiration date.

Extrinsic Value – those aspects of an options pricing that are determined by factors not related to the cost of the equity or security.

Fundamental Analysis - a method of analyzing the intrinsic value of a financial instrument in the stock market and its price value in future.

Hedging – the process of investment that seeks to minimize the risk of trading tour investments.

Historical Volatility – measures an equity's volatility levels through studying past price movements over a period of time.

Horizontal Spread – spread created from several contracts that feature the same strike price and different expiration dates.

Implied Volatility – an estimate of an underlying security's future volatility levels based on current prices, using pricing models.

Index Option –a contract on the options market whose underlying asset is not stock but an index.

In the Money – contract whose stock value s more than the current cost in case of a call position, the opposite is true for a put contract.

Inflation Rate - the percentage in change of either the rice or fall of prices of securities in the stock market.

Inflation - a moment where the prices of securities can either experience a sudden rise or an impromptu fall.

Interest Rate - an amount of interest that paid after a certain amount of time to a stock trader for the money he or she has invested in the stock market.

Interest - this is the amount of money an investor in the stock market receives in turn from the money he or she invests in the stocks purchased.

Intrinsic Value – a contract whose equity value is higher than the strike amount.

Investor - an individual who willingly allocates his or her capital in the stock market with an aim of getting profits in return after a certain amount of time.

Long Position – a position that is created when you purchase a call or put contract.

Leg – individual positions that form up a contract comprising of several positions.

Leverage – the process of using options to obtain more payoffs from the options market.

Limit Order –an order that allows you to trade options at the specified minimum and maximum strike prices.

Limit Stop Order – an order that instructs positions to close when certain prices are attained.

Liquidity - the level of availability of a certain financial instrument. In other words, this is a measure of the level of ease that a certain instrument can be bought or sold without affecting the prices.

Listed Option – an option that is listed on the options market.

Margin Account - a type of brokerage account that an investor give an investor ability to lend cash to customers for them to purchase securities or other financial instruments.

Margin Requirement –this is the amount of money that a trader deposits in his brokerage account to cover for naked option positions. These acts as collateral for the brokerage firm to purchase or sell options on behalf of the trader.

Market Bubble - a situation where prices of stocks are escalated above their actual value by traders.

Market Indicators - formulas and ratios that are able to illustrate the gains and losses in the indexes and stocks.

Market Order – one used to buy or sell a contract at current market prices.

Market Stop Order – the order that closes a position when certain market prices are attained.

Moneyness – a technique used to define the correlation between an equity is underlying cost and the strike amount of an option.

Morphing – the process of creating synthetic positions, or transitioning from one position into another using a single order.

One-Sided Market – market state when buyers are significantly more than sellers, or sellers more than buyers.

Online Brokers – a broker that allows you to process your orders through an online platform.

Opening Order – an order used to create new options contract positions.

Optionable Stock – stock that acts as underlying security for certain options.

Options Contract – a right to purchase or sell shares at specified strike prices and expiration times.

Options Holder – the person who owns an options contract.

Options Trader – a person who buys and sells options.

Out of the Money – an option gets out of the money when the cost of the equity of the underlying security is not favorable to the trader based on the strike price. A call option can become out of the money if the value of the underlying equity is below the strike charges. On the other hand, a put option becomes out of the money when the cost of the underlying equity is higher than the strike charges.

Over the Counter Options – options that are traded over the counter and not through online exchange platforms.

Over Valuing - an occurrence where a stock market trader estimates the prices of stocks to be higher than the actual value in the market.

Portfolio - a grouping of several financial assets such as currencies cash, bonds, stocks and other cash equivalents which are owned by an individual or an organization.

Pricing Model – a formula that can be applied in the determination of the abstract or theoretical value of a given options contract using variables such as the underlying security, strike price, and volatility.

Premium – the amount paid to acquire an option in the options market. Premiums are often quoted as price per share.

Profit - it is the excess revenue a stock trader gets from either buying or selling of stocks in the stock market.

Physical Option – the kind of option that has underlying equity in the form of physical assets.

Put Option – an option that allows you to write or sell underlying equity at a specific strike amount and expiration times.

Realize a Profit - making some profit when you close a position contact.

Realize a Loss – incurring a loss when you close a position contract.

Retail Trader - a person or an organization that is focused in investing their capital in futures, options, bonds and stock.

Risk - it is an unforeseen factor that can lead a stock trader to experience losses while trading in the stock market.

Scaling Out - situation in the stock market where a trader get out of his or her position so as to either buy or sell his or her financial instruments.

Security Index - an indicator in the security market that uses statistical data to analyze the changes that are experienced in the securities market.

Sell to Close Order – order placed when closing a long position that is already in existence.

Sell to Open Order – order placed when opening a new contract position.

Settlement – when contract terms are finalized after exercising a position.

Shares - indivisible form of capital that is used to signify a person's ownership to a certain company.

Short Position – the state attained when you sell contracts.

Short Selling - A phenomena where a stock market investor borrows securities which he or she sells later in the stock market with an aim of making profit by buying them later.

Spread – a position made from selling several contracts belonging to the same underlying security.

Spread Order – an order that instructs a broker to create a spread of several positions that are transacted simultaneously.

Stock Market - a loose network of several traders who willingly buy and sell stocks which represent ownership of certain business.

Stock Options - an agreement agreed by the stock market investor and his or her broker granting the broker exclusive rights to buy or sell shares at a predetermined price.

Stock Trader - an individual or a firm involved in the trading of stocks.

Stock - it is a type of security that gives an individual ownership to certain company and it is sold at a particular market price.

Stop Loss Point - points where a stock trader gives instruction of certain stocks to either be sold or bought when they attain a certain price in the stock market.

Stop Order – An order implemented to close positions from the market when certain price parameters are attained.

Strike Price – the amount of money given or received when a contract holder decides to close a contract position .

Swing Trader – (*definition 1*) a stock trader who holds his or her financial instruments such as stocks for a long time before he or she trades them.

Swing Trader - (*definition 2*) An individual who either buys or sells securities in the market for a period of several days or weeks so as to capture the gains of the market.

Synthetic Position – a trade position that combines options and stocks in a single contract to emulate another option position.

Synthetic Long Call – a synthetic position that allows you to own calls. It entails purchasing puts as well as their related underlying assets.

Synthetic Long Put – a position that allows you to own puts. It entails purchasing calls then short selling the underlying security related with the call.

Synthetic Short Call – a position that is similar to purchasing short calls. Entails selling stocks and selling put options associated with the stock.

Synthetic Short Put – a position that similar to trading short puts. It entails purchasing stock then selling call options associated with the stock.

Synthetic Short Stock – this is a synthetic options position that is similar to going short on stocks. It entails writing one call contract at the money than purchasing one put option that is also at the money for the same underlying stock.

Technical Analysis – a technique used to predict the price of financial instruments such as stocks through analyzing the historical price data of the underlying security.

Theoretical Value – refers to the cost of an option position derived using pricing models and mathematical formulas.

Time Decay – the period when the extrinsic value of an option decreases as it approaches the expiration date.

Trading Plan – this is a plan that traders create to outline how they will carry out transactions on the options market. The plan always contains objectives, trading methods and strategies to be used.

Trailing Stop Order – this is an order whose stop price is a percentage change from the best price ever reached by a given position.

Trading Style – the method used by a trader when transacting on the options market.

Trend – a continuous movement or change in the price of options or market patterns.

Time Value - the time value of any call contract or put contract is the section of the premium that is more in value than the quoted intrinsic value.

Underlying Stock – the kind of security upon which the value of an option is derived.

Under Valuing - a situation where prices of stocks are estimated to be lower than the actual market prices by a stock market trader.

Volatility – the level of rising or falling of the cost of a given option.

Vertical Spread – a combination of options positions established from multiple contracts that feature diverse strike amounts with similar expiry dates.

Volatile Market – an exchange platform that has prices or conditions that keep changing in an unexpected manner.

Volatility Crunch – sudden decline in an option has implied volatility.

Volume – the number of transactions carried out in relation to a certain option or underlying security.

Weekly Option – an option that expires within one week.

Writer – the person who creates contract positions for selling options.

Writing an Option – the act of selling an option contract.

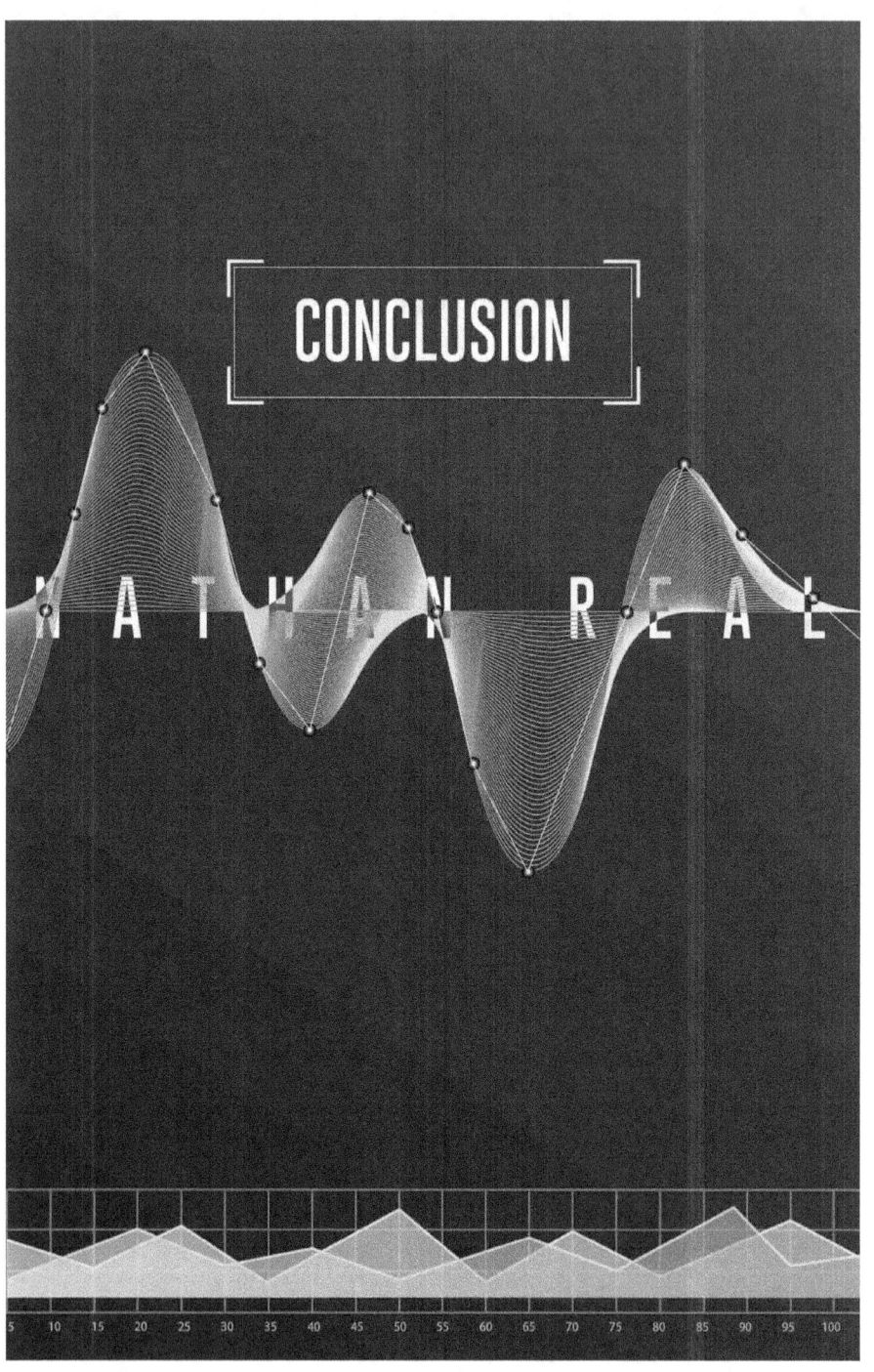

CONCLUSION

Conclusion

With the information you've gained from this book, you are hopefully interested in starting your own account and beginning the process of researching your own trade opportunities. By now you have some foundation from which to do your research as well as a clearer picture of what to expect when choosing a broker and entering your first position.

The research required to be a successful swing trader won't stop when you finish reading this book. Every trade you enter will require another round of reading and studying so that you can choose a position with confidence. Remember what good research consists of; look at the fundamentals of a stock and the history of its performance over time.

Decide if you want to choose a strategy based on the stock or the other way around.

Keep your efforts simple at first, take your time to learn how the market works. As you gain experience your trades will go smoother and you will learn what works and what doesn't. Keep a record of how your trades go. If you continue to swing trade, then over time you will participate in a lot of trades and hold a lot of positions. To learn from them effectively you have got to take notes ad keep track of your progress. You will learn faster if you keep a record.

The amazing thing about trading and competing in the stock market is the sheer number of opportunities available. At any given time, there are new profitable positions that are waiting to be discovered. If you genuinely enjoy reading about new companies and current events, then it will be easier to identify opportunities as they appear.

The other advantage you have currently as a swing trader is the vast network of information available to you. Your stock research is no longer limited to what you can find in a public library and keeping track of the stock market in real-time doesn't require you to be attached to a landline phone. The trends that are hard to reach are more available. Imagine trying to find promising new companies to invest in before the age of the internet. You would have to hear about stock opportunities through sheer luck or knowing the right person.

Now anyone can have access to the information. This means that the market is a lot more competitive, but it also means that there are a lot more opportunities. The internet also provides endless resources to learn strategies and hear what analysts are saying. At the end of the day, take a lot of the noise with a grain of salt. The money you are risking is your own, and you should be leery of the way that certain analysts' opinion can be regarded as fact. Use the information to learn, but always fall back on your own research and intuition at the end of the day.

If you can learn how to trade profitably then you'll be able to enjoy the fruits of a rewarding job. Maybe you will decide to trade more actively and become a day trader. There is nothing wrong with maintaining a balance and swing trading in addition to your normal job. Be honest with yourself about the needs of your lifestyle, and whether your personality is a good match for that kind of path.

Whichever way you choose; whether you decide to continue swing trading or day trading, you'll gain the additional freedom that comes with being your own boss and making money independently for yourself. This is the main reason why people choose to get involved in swing trading; the added flexibility it can offer your life. But, just like any job, it requires work and dedication. Don't be frustrated with yourself if you don't see results right away. Don't think of yourself as a failure or a bad trader if you have a few bad trades. It happens to all of us when we first begin down this path, and it's a part of the learning experience.

If you are still nervous about the prospect of risking your hard-earned money on the stock market, there are other ways for you to gain practice and experience as a trader without risking your money.

Investopedia hosts a stock market simulator that is free to use and available online. When you sign up, the simulator gives you $100,000 of virtual money to use for trading securities. The simulator tracks real stocks from the New York Stock Exchange and all the major stock indexes. The simulator is updated every fifteen minutes so that you are essentially trading in real-time with the stock market simulator.

The simulator even considers the fees charged by brokers, as well as the commissions. When you trade regularly, whether, with real money or virtual money, you will have to keep track of how these fees are affecting your margins. The fees charged by brokers will affect your decision making, as they will always be a factor in the profitability of your trades. The stock market simulator will give you practice in managing these fees.

The only thing missing from the stock simulator is the psychological challenge of dealing with real risk. You will never know how it feels to truly manage risk until you are trading with real money. The main advantage of using a stock trading simulator is that you will be learning the mechanics of trading. This is just as important to be a good trader, and stock market simulators are something you should look into if you are interested in gaining some free experience.

So, if you have a hunch about a company or you can feel the air changing in the stock market but you don't have the capital to invest right now, you can use a stock market simulator to test your theories and learn in the meantime. Learning how to manage trades will give you confidence when it comes to putting your real money to work.

The more you practice and prepare to start swing trading with real money, the more likely you will be to succeed. The reality of swing trading is this; most will fail to make any profits, or they will quit before they have any success. Swing trading is difficult and competitive. You will be in a much better position to succeed if you can continue to research and learn, practicing and solidifying strategies.

You should be constantly reading about the economy and the stock market. Publications like The Economist, the Wall Street Journal and MarketView will be good resources for learning how economic news and developments will impact the performance of the stock market. They will give you a place to start your research on identifying opportunities in the current market conditions. Current events will steer investor confidence and subsequently the movements of stock prices. Even if you don't open an account right away, get in the habit of keeping up with current events and financial news.

Remember that the best way to find opportunities is to research stocks and sectors that you already have a personal interest in. The knowledge you have already is a useful tool for staying ahead of the market. If you have an interest in cars, then you'll probably enjoy reading about automotive companies; what new car models are being introduced and how do you think they will perform? If you have an interest in computers and tech; what types of technology have you read about that you think could be groundbreaking? Out of all the new companies producing these technologies, which ones have the most promising fundamentals, and are more likely to succeed? If you approach to research this way, then you'll no doubt find opportunities for stocks to trade and invest with.

With all of this in mind, I hope that it is clear to you at least that swing trading is not a passive or easy way to make extra money. You must do your research. But if you find sectors that interest you, and you have a natural interest in current events and a keen eye for opportunities then you will be better equipped to succeed.

Take what you learned from this book and continue to build on it. Swing trading is a challenging prospect with many risks. But if you maintain a disciplined strategy it also has its rewards; better financial freedom, independent income, and the ability to control your own schedule to name a few. If you continue to learn then you are more likely to succeed in this ever-changing world of opportunities.

Thank you for reading the book and getting this far! If you liked this book, we invite you to learn more by reading other titles written by Nathan Real:

Options Trading: the Beginner's Guide for Options Trading to Learn Strategies and Techniques, Making Money in Few Weeks.

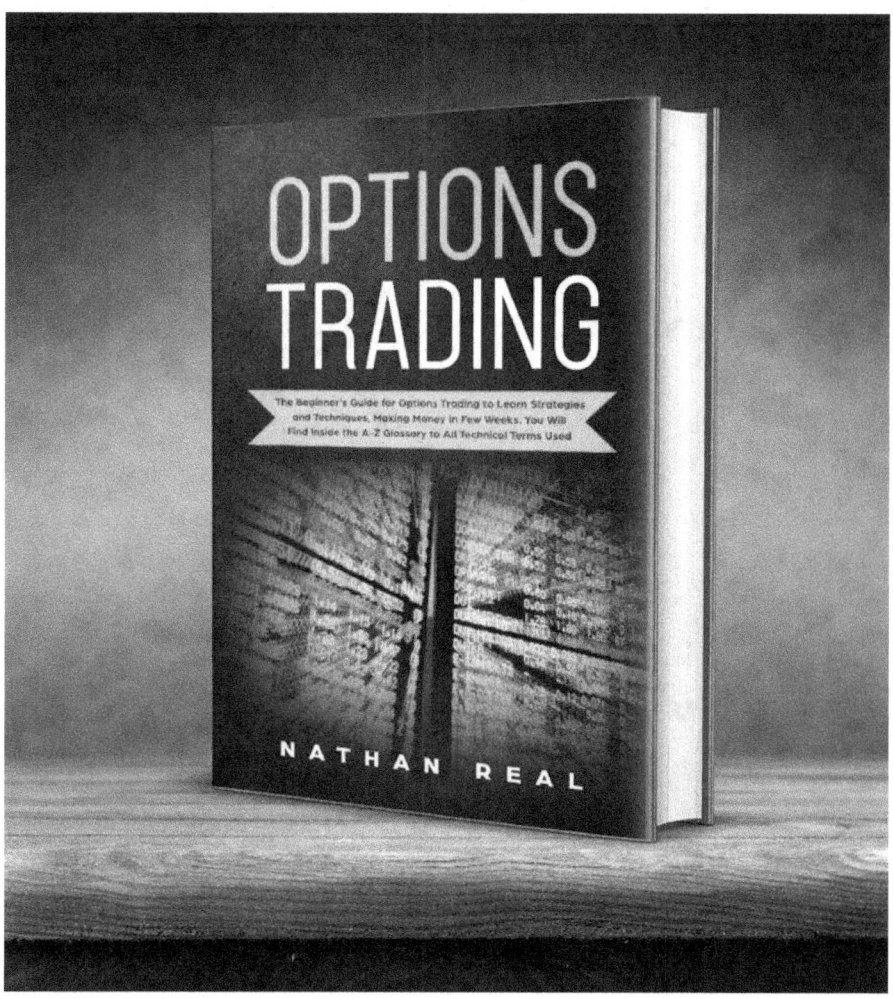

Day Trading Forex: the forex basics Explained with all Trading Strategies. A Proven Method to Become a Profitable Forex Trader.

Stock Trading for Beginners: an Easy Guide to the Stock Market with the Trading Strategy to achieve Financial Freedom.

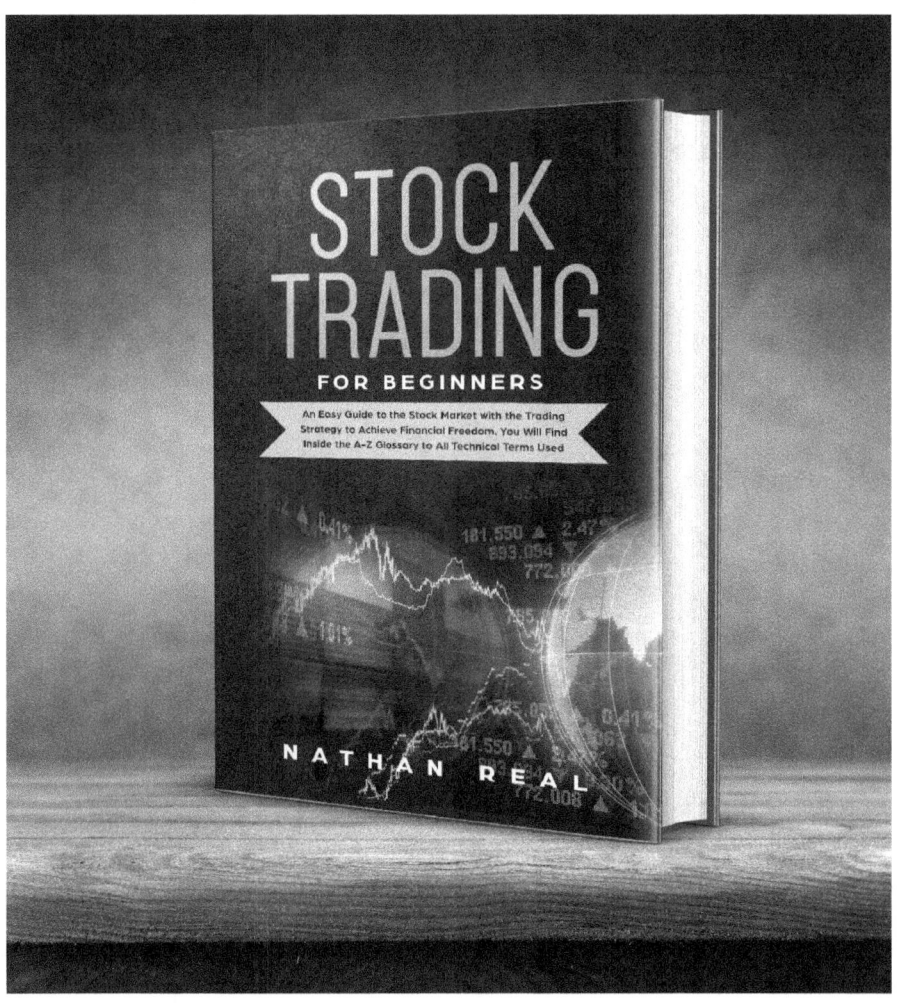

www.ingramcontent.com/pod-product-compliance
Lightning Source LLC
Chambersburg PA
CBHW070346220526
45467CB00001B/261

DAILY SELF DISCIPLINE BLUEPRINT:

A WORKBOOK WITH SUCCESS TRICKS AND POSITIVE HABITS TO ACHIEVE HIGH SELF ESTEEM AND CONFIDENCE. DO BETTER AND IMPROVE YOUR MOTIVATION TO HAVE NO EXCUSES IN YOUR LIFE!

© Copyright 2019 - All rights reserved.

The content contained within this book may not be reproduced, duplicated or transmitted without direct written permission from the author or the publisher.

Under no circumstances will any blame or legal responsibility be held against the publisher, or author, for any damages, reparation, or monetary loss due to the information contained within this book. Either directly or indirectly.

Legal Notice:

This book is copyright protected. This book is only for personal use. You cannot amend, distribute, sell, use, quote or paraphrase any part, or the content within this book, without the consent of the author or publisher.

Disclaimer Notice:

Please note the information contained within this document is for educational and entertainment purposes only. All effort has been executed to present accurate, up to date, and reliable, complete information. No warranties of any kind are declared or implied. Readers acknowledge that the author is not engaging in the rendering of legal, financial, medical or professional advice. The content within this book has been derived from various sources. Please consult a licensed professional before attempting any techniques outlined in this book.

By reading this document, the reader agrees that under no circumstances is the author responsible for any losses, direct or indirect, which are incurred as a result of the use of information